Patriotism

Patriotism

Charles Jones and
Richard Vernon

polity

The right of Charles Jones & Richard Vernon to be identified as Author of this Work has been asserted in accordance with the UK Copyright, Designs and Patents Act 1988.

First published in 2018 by Polity Press

Polity Press
65 Bridge Street
Cambridge CB2 1UR, UK

Polity Press
101 Station Landing
Suite 300
Medford, MA 02155, USA

ISBN-13: 978-1-5095-1832-6
ISBN-13: 978-1-5095-1833-3(pb)

A catalogue record for this book is available from the British Library.

Typeset in 10.5 on 12 pt Sabon
by Toppan Best-set Premedia Limited
Printed and bound in Great Britain by Clays Ltd, St. Ives PLC.

The publisher has used its best endeavours to ensure that the URLs for external websites referred to in this book are correct and active at the time of going to press. However, the publisher has no responsibility for the websites and can make no guarantee that a site will remain live or that the content is or will remain appropriate.

Every effort has been made to trace all copyright holders, but if any have been inadvertently overlooked the publisher will be pleased to include any necessary credits in any subsequent reprint or edition.

For further information on Polity, visit our website:
politybooks.com

Contents

Introduction

While we were writing this book, the topic of patriotism moved suddenly and (to many, at least) unpredictably from the margins of political thought to a place where it demanded attention. Excellent recent work had been done on the topic, to be sure (for example Kleinig et al. 2015); but for a generation or more political theorists had given an unprecedented amount of attention to questions of global justice – to the relative levels of wealth and poverty among nations, to the fairness of international trade and transnational institutions, to immigration and refugee policy, to the limits of state sovereignty, and to questions about international aid. These concerns paralleled real-world phenomena: the globalization of economic relations, international trade agreements, the gradual emergence of international criminal law and of other rule-based conceptions of global order, and of course the evolution of the European Union as a possible more transnational future. While no one could have been unaware of patriotism as a background political fact, to the extent that most political theorists took note of it patriotism would have figured as a constraint rather than as one of the political values defining the concerns of their discipline. As this book was being written, however, the explosive rise of populism in many states generally defined by liberal-democratic values, the manifest dislike on the part of many publics for immigration and globalized interstate relations, and in particular the election of Donald Trump in the

US and the Brexit vote in the UK, all signalled that patriotism could no longer be left in the margin of political thought, but demanded serious attention.

Political theorists typically write (and teach) about concepts such as justice, equality or freedom, that is, concepts that *in the first instance* are not tied to anyone's particular time or place, even though, over the past few decades, the discipline has become very much better at taking account of the ways in which time and place can radically modify the interpretation and application of such concepts. For example, in addition to tackling the ways in which the idea of justice needs to take account of the hugely unequal distribution of benefits and burdens in the world, theorists have addressed the ways in which the idea of equality needs to take account of the differently placed concerns of minority cultural groups, and the ways in which the idea of freedom needs to be explored in terms of its real rather than formal – or positive rather than negative – aspects. So no serious critic could fairly accuse political theorists of the early twenty-first century of disconnection from political reality. But the challenge of patriotism is basic in that it raises the question of what we should take *the first instance* to be. For the (re)emergence of 'America First' politics in the United States, of resistance to transnational institutions in the UK and elsewhere, and of the general questioning of the idea of a rule-based international order in the name of a re-affirmation of national sovereignty, all point in the direction of something that is *in the first instance* particular: the fact of belonging to one political society rather than another. What seemed to be emerging in public discourse, as we wrote this book, was a view that we could no longer think that particularity was simply something that political theorists would need to take account of, eventually, in exploring concepts of universal importance. For if the strongest claims of resurgent patriotism are true – if people are to be seen as, above all, compatriots who share with others of their kind a particular identity, shared interests and a distinctive tradition – then the tables are turned, and universal concepts such as justice, equality and freedom will need to find their place, if they can, within a framework for which they no longer provide the point of departure. That people belong to a particular political society, and attach primary importance to their belonging, may demand attention as a basic political fact.

Although recent events have given prominence to our topic, in this book we take a longer view. While the explosion of patriotic sentiment may have taken political theorists (especially liberal political theorists) by surprise, the tradition of political theory is not exactly without resources in terms of addressing the place of particular loyalty within our normative world. Each of the chapters below examines a distinctive and well-developed approach. All of these approaches deserve attention if the defensibility of patriotism is to be established.

What, though, is patriotism? There is near-consensus on how to define it: every source tells us that it is love of and loyalty to one's country, together with special concern for the well-being of one's compatriots, even though, as we shall see, some details in this formula vary. But that general idea is one that has been filled out in many ways, put to many uses, and both celebrated and reviled from many points of view. We do not attempt to give a history of the idea's uses here: the history is a rich one, for the engagement of people with their homeland, as well as efforts to reinforce that engagement, are such common elements of political life, and the meanings of 'love', 'loyalty' and 'country' are so open to interpretation. To introduce our discussion, we simply begin with three historical examples that, between them, raise many of the themes and issues that this book is to explore: an eighteenth-century sermon, a late-nineteenth-century textbook, and a famous twentieth-century academic lecture.

Republics, flags and ways of life

Our first example is a sermon delivered by Richard Price, 'A Discourse on the Love of Our Country' (1789). Price was a British 'Radical', that is, a member of a group of thinkers and activists who advocated constitutional reforms, and who also – contrary to official British policy – sympathized with the revolutionaries in the former American colonies and, a decade later, in France. Interestingly, Price's sermon combines appeals to two traditions that have been enormously influential for the development of the idea of patriotism, often in conflicting ways. Price begins by invoking an ancient view that is generally attributed to Stoic writers such as Seneca and Cicero. Borrowing from those sources, Price employs a very well-known image, that of concentric circles of association radiating out from the individual: we are connected first with those who are personally close to us, such as family and friends, then with our country, and then with humanity at large. Very much in line with this tradition, Price declares that it is an arbitrary matter that one has been born in a particular place, that 'the soil or spot of earth on which we happen to have been born' has no moral significance, and that it is what we owe to the largest circle of association, humanity itself, that has overriding importance. Nevertheless, 'we are so constituted that our affections are more drawn to some among mankind than to others, in proportion to their degrees of nearness to us, and our power of being useful to them'. He continues, 'We can do little for the interest of mankind at large' (1789: 9–10), and so we should think of our country as the place in which we can most effectively bring to bear what we owe to other people (see Duthille 2012 for discussion).

On this view, although one's country is made out to be a site of duty – a duty of special care to compatriots – we may seem to be at some distance from anything that would normally be called 'love'. We 'happen' to have membership in one country rather than another, and Price warns us against excessive partiality toward it – we are (wrongly) 'disposed to overvalue' its particular features (4). But Price's initial view soon merges with another tradition, one that is often called 'republican', or 'neo-Roman' because its exponents looked back to the Roman republic as an inspirational model. And on this view, a more intense engagement with one's country is demanded. A country is to be valued because it has free political institutions, and maintaining those institutions calls for active participation and vigilance on the part of citizens. They must be 'awake to encroachments' on their freedom (29), and 'anxious' to transmit the blessings of freedom to their descendants (42). What one could be said to 'love' is the spirit of freedom that one's country embodies. In the British context, Price identifies this spirit with the Revolution of 1688, which gave force to the right of liberty of conscience, the right to resist abuse, and the right of a people to choose their governors. Those rights, however, are still incompletely realized (33–4), and so the duty of the patriot is to fight to realize them more fully, by making religious liberty more comprehensive and electoral representation more equal. Patriotic love is, then, a critical love, one aimed at the improvement of the love-object. The upshot of 'love of country', according to Price, turns out to be, essentially, commitment to legal and political reform.

Who, though, can be a patriot on this view? The British, obviously, and, by the time Price is writing, the Americans and the French, whose revolutions he regards as successor events to the English Revolution of 1688. But patriotism, if understood as a zeal for liberty (19), would seem to be impossible in countries whose political institutions and traditions do not harbour that zeal. Price writes: 'What is now the love of his country in a *Spaniard*, a *Turk*, or a *Russian*? Can it be considered as any thing better than a passion for slavery, or a blind attachment to a spot where he enjoys no rights, and is disposed of as if he was a beast?' (6). That seems to allow that the subjects of an oppressive state *can* be patriotic, in some sense, but that, being 'blind', their attachment is of no moral worth, being connected to nothing more than an arbitrary 'spot of earth'. So what Price offers is a powerful but decidedly exclusive conception.

Our second example is a book published under the authority of the Legislature of the State of New York in 1900, entitled *Manual of Patriotism: For Use in the Public Schools of the State of New York*. To what may now seem, to some, a remarkable extent, this substantial book (465 pages) is a sustained and passionate celebration of the symbol of the flag. 'Patriotism is love of country, born of familiarity with its history, reverence for its institutions and faith in its possibilities, and is evidenced by obedience to its laws and respect for its flag' (New York State 1900: i). The book implements an 1898 Act of the New York Legislature that requires, firstly, that every public school in the State be provided with a flag and flagstaff; secondly, that regulations be made for the care of the flag; and, thirdly, that a programme of 'patriotic exercises' be drawn up to accompany the salute to the flag that is to begin each school day.

The *Manual* was published at almost the mid-point of the enormous waves of immigration that transformed society in the United States in the late nineteenth and early twentieth centuries, and what its authors were attempting makes immediate sense in that context. They were trying to foster attachment to a political symbol, one that embodied a national history, as a way of assimilating people of different cultures. While there are recurrent references to freedom as a value, the emphasis does not fall, as in Price's sermon, on a constitutional ideal, but on a national story or epic, told by way of 'noble utterances ... [and] vivid pictures of great deeds and patriotic sacrifices' (ii). In line with the editor's view that 'much repetition and constant reiteration' is the only way to transmit strong beliefs, the story is recapitulated not only through the lives of major figures such as Washington and Lincoln but through almost daily anniversaries of important events. The seventy pages that list the anniversaries convey relentless optimism, and on the few occasions on which events of a negative kind are noted, the negativity is instantly mitigated. The Civil War, of course, poses a problem in this regard, but the *Manual* provides stage directions for a tableau whereby students enact the drama of reconciliation, to be followed by a reading of 'The Blue and the Gray' (146–7), a sentimental poem that is entirely silent on either the war's origin in the slavery issue or its actual outcome for former slaves.

If Price's sermon offers critical patriotism, the *Manual* offers what we may term celebratory patriotism. It has many of the features of a civil religion (even though, interestingly, the explicit invocation of God in the daily pledge was not to be added until half a century later). The daily exercises are termed 'observances', and they are to reach 'the very souls' of the students. The language of 'reverence' in connection with the flag, the hymn-like songs, the memorization of formulas, the rituals of commitment, and the list of anniversaries somewhat mimicking a sacred calendar, all tend to convert the schoolroom into a secular church. If Price is to be faulted, as one contemporary critic immediately alleged, for his austerely instrumental view of the state, for exaggerating the appeal of the 'general' at the expense of the 'local', and for neglecting the 'heart' in favour of 'refined' principle (Coxe 1790: 8–12), then the *Manual* would surely provoke different worries altogether: worries about what happens when the critical faculties are blunted in the interests of belonging.

Our third example is a lecture by the political philosopher Alasdair MacIntyre, 'Is Patriotism a Virtue?' (1984). MacIntyre's lecture actually takes the form of a confrontation between liberal political theory and patriotism of a communitarian kind, but since he gives the communitarian the last word in the exchange it seems legitimate to suppose that his sympathies eventually settle on one side. The view that he concludes by rejecting clearly resembles the first of Price's models, described above as (broadly) 'Stoic'. This is the view that one can satisfactorily conceive of a country as, basically, a local container for universal beliefs; that in principle all moral duties are duties to human beings as such, but for contingent reasons they have to be restricted in their scope of application. What that view fatally neglects, MacIntyre claims, borrowing a Hegelian term, is the morality of *Sittlichkeit*, that is, the whole accumulated weight of traditions, customs, narratives and memories that one inherits as a member of a political society and which shape one's understanding of it. It is a fundamental error to neglect this, MacIntyre argues, for three reasons. First, moral learning is always local learning, that is, it takes place in interaction and dialogue with specific others with whom one has specific kinds of relationship. Second, the content of what is learned is always local, and is coloured with specific ideas of the good. Third, behaving well is hard, and is possible only because the standards of behaving well are reinforced by membership in a community in which common standards are upheld. To suppose that we can become good by learning what is due to all humans indifferently is, then, to ignore the actual source of moral development. (We discuss these claims critically in Chapter 1 below.)

The New York State *Manual*, we noted above, was intended to encourage the political integration of people from many different ethnicities and backgrounds, and for that reason developed political rather than cultural symbolism. MacIntyre's view of the role of patriotism, however, goes deeper.

One's country is taken to be an all-encompassing source of identity rather than simply a shared point of political reference. Its narrative is *not* something distinct from the varied cultural identities in an immigrant society but something to which one's own personal identity is connected. 'Each one of us to some degree or other understands his or her life as an enacted narrative ... A central contention of the morality of patriotism is that I will obliterate and lose a central dimension of the moral life if I do not understand the enacted narrative of my own individual life as embedded in the history of my country' (1984: 16).

MacIntyre denies, importantly, that patriotism as he understands it is uncritical: here he is closer to Price's view that love of country may provide a basis for criticizing its policies than he is to the much more purely celebratory style of the *Manual*. He points out, for example, that a particular conception of what it meant to be German could lead people to find the Nazi regime deeply dishonourable, and destructive of what was taken to be essential to German nationality – a critical viewpoint distinct from the 'disputable, at worst cloudy rhetoric' of appealing to 'the best interests of mankind' (14). Moreover, being part of a society entails taking ownership of its past wrongs and responsibility for making good, and thus calls for a sober understanding of its history. If I do not understand my life as embedded within my country's history, I will not understand 'for what crimes of my nation I am bound to make reparation' (16).

On the other hand, the claims that MacIntyre makes for asserting one's nationhood are more robust than we find in either of the two earlier examples. For Price, the only just war is a war of defence against external aggression (1789: 29). The *Manual* appears to add to this another permitted war, a war of liberation to free oppressed peoples from imperial control, representing the Spanish-American War in this light (New York State 1900: 197–202). MacIntyre's lecture, however, admits a forthright appeal to national interest: 'What your community requires as the material prerequisites for your survival as a distinctive community and your growth into a distinctive nation may be exclusive use of the same or some of the same natural resources as my community requires for its survival', and, recognizing this, we must therefore endorse 'a willingness to go to war on one's community's behalf' (1984: 6). In the last resort, then, patriotism will be incompatible with an 'impersonal' or impartial standpoint that assigns equal value to all humans, and any proposed moderate patriotism that limits what we owe to our country in the name of some universal values would be untenable. For engagement with one's country's way of life – and hence one's own moral identity – may eventually require defending the resources that alone make it possible.

What to make of patriotism? Four initial questions

Here, then, we have three cases in which (some version of) patriotism is strongly articulated, but in which the 'country' that we are to love, what it means to 'love' it and what we owe to our 'compatriots' are all differently defined. So let us briefly survey some salient differences, simply as a way of framing the issues to be taken up in this book.

Content

The most straightforwardly political conception is, obviously, Richard Price's. Patriotism is the defence of a political value, understood (according to the dominant strand in his thinking) as a constitutional regime with civil freedoms and equal political representation. The bare fact that this freedom is *ours* is, morally speaking, beside the point, except to the (significant) extent that it falls to us to defend it. The freedom in question is to serve as a critical standpoint from which to evaluate domestic policy, and foreign policy to the extent that this involves relations with other free polities, such as revolutionary America and France. The conception of political institutions involved is strictly instrumental, as we can see from the austerely non-reverential forms of address that Price recommends (1789: 23–7). We have already noted the contrast with the New York State *Manual*, distinctly thin on principle, really strong on reverence, and constructed around a symbol that encapsulates an epic national story, while Mac-Intyre's epic narrative is more all-embracing. It is a narrative that underwrites one's moral and cultural identity, and one's 'country' is understood not as the geographical locus of a principle, *nor* as (only) a political nation, but as nothing less than an identity-creating way of life. Some recent political thought, in what is termed the liberal nationalist vein, attempts to distinguish a public culture, which governs the way in which a political society creates itself by collective action over time, from broader notions of culture such as 'Englishness' or 'Frenchness', notions relating to the fine-grained informal protocols that regulate everyday life (Miller 1995: 172–3). But MacIntyre's approach does not offer us that distinction: our country defines who we are, not just the way in which we conduct our public business.

Function

Our three texts assume that patriotism does different things. For Price and the republican tradition (to be discussed in Chapter 3), it inspires and motivates civil vigilance, the sense that freedom requires our active support against tyranny. It has given rise to the three great revolutions that have made political freedom possible. For the *Manual*, it is the one belief that can attract support for a strong sense of belonging in a new world, among people who would otherwise have no world in common. The book therefore provides a vivid example of the important role of patriotism in the nation-building projects of the nineteenth century. In MacIntyre's case the term 'function' seems bloodlessly inadequate to what is claimed, for patriotism is nothing less than the motivational set that makes our moral life and even our identity possible. We cannot regard it as merely instrumental.

Limits

The spectrum in this regard runs from Price's first or 'Stoic' conception at one end to MacIntyre's robust and potentially aggressive conception at the other, one that recognizes

zero-sum conflicts and licenses the desire to make the resulting sum positive for oneself. Offering a hope that Americans
will be friendly to the freedom of other countries – a hope
that would seem to preclude certain kinds of foreign policy –
the *Manual* occupies a rather uninformative middle ground.
If one's country is to be understood as a place in which (what
we may term) human rights may effectively be promoted,
then there is no basis for giving preference to promoting
our compatriots' human rights if and when, as it happened,
we could more effectively promote the rights of outsiders;
and it is not hard to imagine situations in which that choice
would arise. Suppose, for example, human subsistence rights
include access to water, and we have enough while others do
not – there would be no moral basis for holding on to what
we have at the others' expense. But MacIntyre's lecture, as
we have seen, points to a different answer: we may protect
the material conditions of our way of life, and the view that
we would not in the last resort be entitled to protect them
misunderstands the very idea of patriotism.

'Our' country

We have already noted the attenuated sense in which Price's
patriotism is about 'our' country, as opposed to a convenient
locus in which duties (either Stoic or republican, depend-
ing on which theme we emphasize) may be discharged, and
we have noted, too, the kind of objection to which such a
view is exposed. The 'spot of earth' which we inhabit, as an
early critic (Coxe 1790) notes, cannot readily be separated
from the sense of belonging that people typically have, as
we can also see from the role that physical geography (as
distinct from political philosophy) often plays in national
anthems. The *Manual*, on the other hand, as was also noted
above, is perhaps best understood in this respect as *making*
'us', that is, in setting out to appeal to and capture the
loyalty of people with diverse backgrounds, it provides a
rallying-point for the sentiment of solidarity. It expresses a
project for creating citizens, as distinct from the project of
drawing out what, from a moral point of view, citizenship
should entail.

But it is what MacIntyre means by 'our' country that is most challenging and provocative. He rightly points out that it makes no sense to say that one is 'patriotic' about a country other than one's own: one may admire German music or French culture even if one is not German or French, but only German or French people can be said to be *patriotic* about those things. We can be patriotic only about what is ours. But this is different from what Price would term a 'blind attachment', for what we are patriotic about are the discernible 'achievements' of our country – so the attachment is not content-free. Indeed, if it were content-free, that would in fact make it impossible for patriotism to have the potentially critical role that MacIntyre claims for it, since it must contain something against which policies and regimes could be measured and found wanting. But that leads to what may be the deepest puzzle in MacIntyre's view, and perhaps in all strong defences of patriotism. No doubt our country has many achievements in its past. But why is recognizing those achievements more appropriate than recognizing the achievements of other countries? Is it because we claim to have done things better than them, or that what we have done well at is better than what other countries have done well at? Is it like some cricket-playing nation claiming to be best of all at cricket, or, alternatively, like the Irish claiming that hurling (which they alone play) is the best sport of all? Whether we have succeeded at something more than other countries have, or whether what we do is more valuable than what other countries do, are better understood as deep and hard-to-answer questions than as the basis of any assumption. As Price remarked, while we esteem our own country, 'in other countries [there may be] as much of all that deserves esteem' (1789: 4). So if we simply assume that our achievements have some special loyalty-attracting importance, and one that is not to be exposed to some kind of dispassionate comparative assessment, are we not back to valuing what is ours simply *because* it is ours?

Two things are essential, it would seem, to a defensible patriotism. One is that it should include some reflectively defensible values, if it is not to fall into the category of merely prejudiced assumption ('blind patriotism'). The other is that it should assign moral weight to the contingent fact that the values or value-charged stories are our own. Is that possible? Or does the attachment to what is ours necessarily corrupt or foreclose on the reflective assessment of values?

Let us return to the *Manual* for what may be a telling example of the tension here. In its celebratory approach to patriotic identity, it has to make the best of the violence in the country's past, and it does so, as we saw, by celebrating the Civil War as the avenue to achieving a hard-fought but eventually harmonious consensus on racial equality. In doing so, it becomes complicit in a national mythology that derived its 'enormous consoling power' from drawing a veil over the continuation of 'massive racial oppression' in the post-war South, endorsing what one moral philosopher rightly terms a fantasy – 'the fantasy that all had turned out well enough after all' (Callan 2010: 268). Callan's judgement is supported by historical research on the ways in which the post-bellum South re-created slavery in all but name (Blackmon 2009).

Is this kind of self-deception, as (we shall see) some maintain, an inevitable consequence of patriotism? Or is there a reflective version of patriotic belief that escapes the trap? And is there a version of patriotism that accepts reasonable limits to its demands without ignoring the real sources of patriotic feeling, or, alternatively, collapsing into something so diluted – and so remote from what, as a matter of fact, attaches people to their country and mobilizes them in its support – that it should hardly be called patriotism at all? If we evaluate our country on some scale or other, must we be self-critically open to disappointment if it falls short – thus ceasing to be patriots? Or, if we do not measure it comparatively, are we open to charges of irrationality? In this book we work our way toward a cautiously positive view.

Here is a chapter-by-chapter summary of our plan. Chapter 1 considers patriotism as a case of the broader notion of 'associative' connections, connections that, like family or friendship, are taken both to ground and to limit people's moral responsibilities. Along the way we address the meaning and value of community, loyalty and partiality as they relate to patriotic attachments. Chapter 2 turns to the more specific view that love of country should be seen in terms of attachment to a 'nation', defined by a shared history and culture; and it considers the claims that might be made for national membership in light of more general human obligations. Chapter 3 introduces a rival and more purely political approach, one that rejects nationalism in favour of a 'republican' tradition that connects patriotism with loyalty to, and alert defence of, free political institutions. Chapter 4 considers the case for giving preference to our compatriots for reasons seen as just requirements of political association itself, as an organization that coercively allocates benefits and burdens to its members. Finally, in our Conclusion – adopting the term 'subsidiarity' – we outline a moderate version of patriotism, one that accepts wider moral constraints, and defend that view from some vigorous representative critiques.

1
Community, Loyalty and Partiality

'All morality is tribal morality ...'

Andrew Oldenquist (1982: 178)

'I love America more than any other country in the world, and, exactly for this reason, I insist on the right to criticize her perpetually.'

James Baldwin (1955: 9)

In the Introduction we attempted to clarify the meaning of patriotism and to offer some initial thoughts on assessing its moral and political status. Our present task is to introduce three large themes around which to consider in more detail what it means to be a patriot and how patriotism measures up to ethical scrutiny. The themes are community, loyalty and partiality. We will address three sets of questions. First, is patriotism a desirable form of community attachment that every person needs in order to live a meaningful life? Second, is the fact that patriotism is a form of loyalty sufficient to give it significant ethical weight? And third, does the partiality of patriotic commitment render it morally questionable? Should we worry that an impartial viewpoint seems to be both morally necessary yet impossible for a true patriot to adopt?

Community, identity and patriotic attachment

Associative duties

We all participate in special relationships of various kinds – within families, with friends, with fellow workers, with co-participants in social causes, and with compatriots – that involve commitments that give our lives both a focus and an identity. To be committed in these ways is to be willing to pursue certain goals and to make sacrifices along the way. It is widely believed that members of certain normatively important social groups – families, friends, colleagues and compatriots – owe fellow members special duties. Samuel Scheffler has coined the label 'associative duties' for these special responsibilities we often recognize toward associates in the various communities to which we belong (Scheffler 2001: 4, 49–65). On this common-sense view, to be a member of one of these communities is to be required to act on the associative duties that members recognize they have toward each other.

Associative duties should be distinguished from two other types of duty: natural and transactional. We owe natural duties, like the duty not to harm others, to every person without reference to any association or community to which we belong. Transactional duties, on the other hand, originate in actions we perform, such as promises or contracts: here a person's duty follows from a voluntary commitment or agreement they make. Our focus here is on associative relationships, which make essential reference to specific groups to which we belong and do not necessarily depend on any voluntary action on our part. For example, we do not choose our parents and, while we can to some extent choose our friends (if they accept our choice), we can but mainly do not choose our country.

Notice that it is one thing to say that it is permissible to favour associates over non-associates, but another thing to say that such favouritism is morally obligatory (Scheffler 2001: 79; Primoratz, in Kleinig et al. 2015: 83). To speak of associative duties is to highlight their obligatory or morally required status: on this view, we are obligated to show special concern for members of certain communities to which we belong. In order to evaluate patriotism we must first recognize that it commits us not merely to allowing special concern but also to demanding that we favour compatriots. How could such stringent requirements be justified? Are we correct in thinking that membership in a particular country or nation-state should be so morally salient that it will properly play a central role in our practical deliberations by creating special duties to our compatriots? (Stilz 2009: 3).

Suppose my affiliation with my country matters to me. Does it follow that I may legitimately privilege my compatriots over non-compatriots in thought and action? If I feel that I belong to my country or have a strong connection to it, why should I conclude based on these feelings that I am morally required to show favouritism toward my compatriots? One answer appeals to the values of community and identity: my country is special because it is the community that gives me the values with which I identify, values that give me an identity and enable me to live a worthwhile life.

Community, identity and morality

As we saw in the Introduction, Alasdair MacIntyre claims that the morality of patriotism corresponds to a communitarian conception of morality according to which 'the questions of *where* and *from whom* I learn my morality turn out to be crucial for both the content and the nature of moral commitment'. Who I am, my sense of my own identity, is tightly linked to the 'particular community' in which I was raised and to which I belong (MacIntyre 1984: 8). If I am patriotic I love an intergenerational community of which I am a part, a community that makes me the person I am. We simply cannot understand ourselves as individuals without situating ourselves within the historical narrative our community shapes for us. For MacIntyre, we must take our 'moral starting point' for understanding our duties from the particular roles we play in these unfolding stories, as daughter, son, mother, father, friend, teacher, citizen, national and patriot. We can know what to do only if we know the narratives in which we play our part (MacIntyre 1981: 216). Similarly, for Michael Sandel, there is a sense of community uniting members of society in which 'community describes not just what they *have* as fellow citizens but also what they *are*, not a relationship they choose (as in a voluntary association) but an attachment they discover, not merely an attribute but a constituent of their identity' (Sandel 1982: 150). Sandel claims that our identity is bound up with our 'aims and attachments', our basic allegiances that demand loyalty to particular others while at the same time making us the particular people we are. The reality of our 'moral experience' requires that we view ourselves 'as members of this family or community or nation or people, as bearers of this history, as sons and daughters of that revolution, as citizens of this republic' (179). In short, identity comes with its own implications for our moral allegiances, including duties to our compatriots.

MacIntyre and Sandel are correct that our social roles set the stage for determining our moral duties to others. When considering associative duties – to family, friends, compatriots – we cannot avoid addressing the expectations set for anyone who fills the role in question. The problem with their analysis, however, is that this account of 'role morality' places too much emphasis on discovering our roles rather than deciding what they should be and what duties follow from inhabiting them. We do not have clearly defined duties that follow directly from our assigned station; instead we cannot avoid making difficult decisions about what to do, as a parent, friend or fellow citizen (Feinberg 1988: 117). There is a relationship between community and identity, but it is not that we simply discover our communal identities as a sort of destiny; rather we can choose to use our reasoning capacities to shape our identities to a significant extent (Sen 2006: 32–9). In the end it is up to us to decide how prominently to place our love and loyalty to our country within the range of sympathetic commitments we recognize.

Amartya Sen describes what is to be said for having a deep sense of communal identity (Sen 2006: 1–5, 18–23). Sharing an identity with our compatriots can produce emotionally strong bonds that help us overcome the temptation to act in our individual self-interest. Consider also the consequent harm that is done by attempting to understand human conduct while disregarding the fact that we identify with particular others and attach value to our social identities.

It is important to recognize that we are social animals whose development depends on shared communal resources such as language, customs and culture. There is little doubt that human beings need to belong to communities if they are to avoid being detached from sources of meaning and value in their lives. To be affiliated with others seems to be a condition of living a life with a range of interests and commitments in which individuals feel connected to others rather than cut off from them. Yet at the same time the communities to which we belong can be suffocating and damaging to our social and moral development. So if we want to avoid both being isolated and lonely on the one hand, and being herded into an oppressive group on the other, we should seek integration on fair terms with others (Feinberg 1988: 118). In this way, we can have the benefits of social membership while avoiding the loss of individuality it sometimes threatens. At the level of one's country, the national community that merits its members' loyalty should affirm this ideal of integration while recognizing that its members, given their social nature, will belong to many other communities – family, friends, religious, academic, work-related – beneath and beyond the country level. Memberships in some of these communities overlap, but others do not, so the plurality of any person's affiliations is a fact to be registered and a potential source of conflicting commitments. And it should be emphasized that strong communal identities, especially those produced in ways that exclude others, can generate conflict between communities leading all the way up to all-out war. Despite the value of social identities, they can be dangerous because in-group solidarity often combines with hostility toward outsiders. As Sen puts it, a 'strong – and exclusive – sense of belonging to one group can in many cases carry with it the perception of distance and divergence from other groups. Within-group solidarity can help to feed between-group discord' (Sen 2006: 1–2).

Miller on community identity

But it could still be said that ethical thought must have a fundamental place for our community identities, including most prominently our sense of patriotism. David Miller rejects what he calls 'ethical universalism' in part because its emphasis on generic human characteristics (e.g., neediness) or capacities (e.g., for making choices) fails to accept any basic role for relational facts, such as that I am a father or husband or member of a nation, in conceiving the structure of ethical thinking (Miller 1995: 50). In particular, he objects to the way universalist thinking makes an implausibly strong separation between moral agency and both personal identity and moral motivation. What Miller has in mind is that universalists focus on abstract, general, rationally defensible claims such as the promotion of human happiness, with the consequence that they fail to allow any role in ethical thinking for 'considerations about who I am, where I have come from, or which communities I see myself as attached to' (57).

Two replies to Miller seem in order. The first asserts that, contrary to Miller's claim, as ethical agents we are not required to abstract ourselves 'from all social particularity' (MacIntyre 1984: 12, cited in Miller 1995: 57). Rather we need to retain the capacity to abstract from any particular source of identity – say, as parent, friend or citizen – in order to evaluate the demands on us. These demands include not only those arising out of our particular associational memberships but also more general considerations that include taking account of those outside our in-group. The second reply is that where we begin our ethical thinking is less important than how we engage in it. If we start from a universalist standpoint, recognizing the demand to promote human happiness or protect basic human rights, this does not rule out taking account of associative duties to family, friends or compatriots. And if we begin from a particularist standpoint, asking what is required of a compatriot in a given situation, this does not allow us to overlook our duties to our fellow human beings or to accede to the received view about the relative strength of these competing sources of motivation.

Moral values as community values

How much critical judgement can patriots display? (Nathanson 1993: 93). Michael Walzer argues that the only sort of critical commentary that should be taken seriously is the attentive criticism that comes from insiders, so-called 'engaged' or connected critics (Walzer 1987, 1988). We can imagine at least two reasons, epistemic and motivational, why this claim might seem well founded. First, community insiders are more likely to know the social and historical context in which their country finds itself. In short, their knowledge gives others reason to take them seriously. Second, true insiders are presumably motivated by love for their country, so their compatriots are unlikely to doubt that they want what is best for it. But suppose someone voices criticism of their country's policies or actions by appealing to allegedly universal moral values. One way of rejecting such criticism is by claiming that values themselves are relative to communities so that appealing beyond them to the wider world involves a misunderstanding of what it means to evaluate one's community.

We can distinguish two versions of the communitarian claim that moral values are community values: descriptive and normative. The descriptive version says that this is simply what values are, namely, any norms we understand and accept will be those of our community. If values come from outside, they are not our values. Since this claim purports to describe the world as it is, it is worth pointing out that it is false. First, consider the difference between moral development and moral acceptability. We learn about values through a process of moral education in which the lessons of our particular traditions play a crucial role. To become a morally mature person is to participate in this learning process, to listen to moral authorities, and to come to accept core values handed down to us. (Even this account of moral development can be questioned: we do not – and should not – simply accept what is handed down to us.) But it is one thing to describe how we come to possess our moral perspective on the world; it is quite another to suggest that this story prevents us from objecting to our community's practices by appealing to any values we think relevant. We can bracket aspects of our moral views and subject them to criticism whose source lies beyond our community's boundaries. The second reason to question the claim that values always come from within a given community is that there is no community whose values are universally accepted by its members;

every society is characterized by internal disagreement about fundamental matters of morality. Consequently, there can be nothing to which we can point when identifying *our* values, and there is no substitute for entering the conversation by learning the arguments on different sides and considering matters for oneself.

The normative version of communitarianism about values says our values are the ones we *should* accept: if some moral ideal comes from beyond our borders, on this view we should reject it as alien or unsuitable for our own moral circumstances. Morality is our community's morality. But there are several difficulties with this view. First, which community should we take seriously? Why should we think that our country or nation is the only source of acceptable moral claims for us? What about our parents, our loved ones, our ethnic group or our religious tradition? In fact, what about absolutely any person or tradition in so far as they provide a reasonable and attractive case for their claims? Second, and following from the first point, we should notice that moral conflicts are inevitable. When loyalty to my friends or parents or children conflicts with loyalty to my country, which side should prevail? E. M. Forster wrote that 'if I had to choose between betraying my country and betraying my friend, I hope I should have the guts to betray my country' (Forster 1939: 8). Writing in 1939 as the world headed toward large-scale war, Forster worried that personal loyalties were threatened by commitment to patriotic attachment and the violence it promised. In general terms, however, Forster's view is too simplistic to settle the relative merits when loyalties conflict. In the historical context of the threat of fascism and war in Europe in 1939, a strong case could be made for British patriotism – for not betraying one's country – as a necessary part of the anti-fascist struggle (and even for German patriotism to resist Nazism in the name of their country's ideals). The point, however, is that moral conflicts exist, including conflicts of loyalties. It is unproductive and unrealistic to think that moral conflict resolution will be easy. Instead, an appeal to patriotism is only one starting point in a difficult but necessary discussion in which reasons are exchanged, objections raised, responses offered, and perhaps compromise achieved. In this messy reality, no solution is achieved by a simple appeal to love of country.

Loyalty

Patriotic loyalty

Rose Mary Woods was personal secretary to Richard Nixon from his days as a new US congressman in 1950 through his time as US president from 1969 to 1974. She is best known as an exemplar of loyalty because she stuck by Nixon through his public disgrace, refusing to divulge any incriminating information about his misdeeds and even erasing part of a potentially revealing audiotape during the Watergate investigation (though she claimed to have done so inadvertently). Woods was loyal to Nixon even as it became clear to all that he had been involved in illegal actions and the ensuing cover-up. 'People should be loyal', said Woods, 'or else they shouldn't take those jobs. Would *you* want someone working for you and learning all about you who wasn't loyal?' (Gates 1998: 44). As the example of Rose Mary Woods shows, to be loyal to someone is to support them even when doing so incurs costs to one's self-interest or commitment to laws, rules or principles. One can be loyal to many sorts of people, including family members, friends, colleagues or compatriots. To be loyal to a person or group is to show them special concern, to be partial to them, and to be willing to make sacrifices for their sake. To be loyal is to value the relationship intrinsically rather than instrumentally (Scheffler 2001: 100). But loyalty is not always desirable: 'a person who is loyal to the Nazi party is truly loyal, but it would be better if he were not'. To think that loyalty is valuable 'just because it is loyalty' is a mistake (Keller 2007: 152). A key question for us, then, is whether our membership in various associations is such that we are obligated to value them for their own sake and, if so, why. Is being a patriot more like being loyal to your friend or like being true to your fellow racists?

Patriotism is often defended by being characterized as an instance of the virtue of loyalty. For John Kleinig, 'loyalty is the virtue of sticking with and supporting an associative object in the face of narrowly self-serving temptation' (Kleinig et al. 2015: 22). When the object of loyalty is one's country, we have patriotism, which is not merely love of country but 'constancy in love of country' (Callan 2010: 253), perseverance in support of it. It is reliable when times get tough, when personal sacrifice is called for, and when self-interest threatens to pull us in a different direction. A patriot recognizes a special relationship to her country that consists in emotional attachment and an inclination to side with it and act to support it (Keller 2007: 21).

A central feature of patriotic loyalty is the commitment to make sacrifices for your country when its legitimate interests are threatened or when it is not living up to its self-expressed ideals. As US President John F. Kennedy said in his famous 1961 inaugural address, 'so, my fellow Americans: ask not what your country can do for you – ask what you can do for your country'. The emphasis here is not on receiving benefits but on acting in the name of your country to help promote its interests and achieve its ideals. And it is worth noting that Kennedy's rarely quoted next sentence identifies one such ideal: 'My fellow citizens of the world: ask not what America will do for you, but what together we can do for the freedom of man' (Kennedy 1961). The idea is that we are all world citizens regardless of our membership in any particular country and that all of us can and should cooperate in promoting human freedom. Patriotism, on this view, is not only consistent with universal values such as freedom; it is a vital means to securing those values.

My country, right or wrong

If loyalty to one's country is a virtue, this could be due to the value for people of acting on their affection and concern for their compatriots. But now consider whether it is defensible to be loyal regardless of what one's country has done or is proposing to do. George Fletcher claims that '[l]oyalties generally lead people to suspend judgment about right and wrong' (Fletcher 1993: 36), but it is a substantive moral question whether being loyal means offering unquestioning allegiance.

We often interpret loyalty in friendship and family relationships as demanding that we use our critical moral intelligence. What about patriotic loyalty? The famous phrase, 'My country, right or wrong', suggests that the brute fact that it is *my* country provides sufficient reason to support it without having to decide whether its history or proposed plans are morally acceptable. The source for this phrase is a toast made in 1816 by the American naval officer, Stephen Decatur: 'Our country! In her intercourse with foreign nations, may she always be in the right; but our country, right or wrong' (Knowles 2004: 261). If Decatur meant that we should be patriotic without regard to the rightness of our country's cause at a particular time, this implies that patriots should unquestioningly accept their country's policies and actions simply because they are those of their country. But apart from assuming that special value attaches to something's being 'mine', this attitude is unwise for at least three reasons. First and most obviously, it would prevent evaluating the ethical merits of what one's country is proposing to do. Second, it fails to distinguish the current government's plans on the one hand from the country's interests on the other. Governments can be mistaken; when they are, patriotic concern should motivate citizens to point out what is wrong and how the government's policy can be improved. A patriot is committed to promoting her country's welfare and working for change when she judges it is headed in the wrong direction (Barry 1991: 209). Third, uncritical acceptance of one's own country's actions makes it more likely that such actions will, in the end, harm one's country. So, if patriots aim to promote their country's interests, blind support can lead to the opposite outcome from the intended one.

Accordingly, instead of the simplistic motto, 'My country, right or wrong', a much more promising slogan is the one stated in 1872 by the German-American US Senator, Carl Schurz: 'My country, right or wrong; if right, to be kept right; and if wrong, to be set right!' (Knowles 2004: 672). Here the idea is that, for a patriot, the focus is 'my country': I care about this country because it is mine, but my concern is not uncritical. As James Baldwin suggests in this chapter's epigraph, love of one's country should motivate criticism of it. I want the country I love to be a source of pride rather than guilt and shame, so I should be motivated to help ensure it achieves valuable goals and to put it on the right track when its policies seem to me misguided or otherwise wrong. The point is that patriots should always ask whether their country is proposing to do something morally permissible. If so, then loyal support is legitimate; if not, then loyalty demands that citizens work toward putting their country on the right track. In neither case is blind support permitted. Critical concern about British foreign policy can account for a British patriot's shame about its colonial record or pride in its response to Nazi aggression (Caney 2008: 512). This idea of critical concern is nicely expressed by Kwame Anthony Appiah, who understands patriotism as 'having to do with a sense of investment in the national honour. I think that caring about what your country is doing in the world – feeling bad when it does bad things and good when it does good things – that is at the heart of the kind of morally appropriate patriotism that I think is a decent thing' (Appiah 2016).

Consider the role of moral emotions such as pride or shame in our lives. It could be argued that it is only toward your own country, rather than the entire human race, that you can feel pride or shame; so patriotic attachment is a precondition for an emotionally coherent human life. But beyond pointing out that we can feel pride or shame in human conduct in general (say, pride in the human ingenuity displayed in reducing the threat of disease or shame in our infliction of suffering on non-human animals), even so the moral universalist can reply that it is your country's fulfil-ment or denial of *universal* values, like justice or freedom, that gives rise to pride or shame at all. If so, we seem to be led to recognize the value of both patriotic affiliation and universal values. But the vital point here is that the primary role in explaining and justifying our moral emotions is played by general human values rather than country-specific ones.

In fact, the word 'country' obscures a distinction between three possible objects of loyalty: (1) the institutions of power, including the state and its constitutional framework; (2) the current government, as in the people who now hold power; and (3) the group of compatriots who usually share a sense of nationality (Nathanson 1993: 124–6). Loyalty to one of these three does not require loyalty to either of the others. In fact, resistance to the current government can be motivated by loyalty to my compatriots together with a shared respect for constitutional ideals like freedom and equality to which we take ourselves to be committed. Without these distinctions, we cannot know whether any claim about patriotic loyalty is legitimate because there is not yet any identifiable object of loyalty.

Can patriotism be a virtue?

Alasdair MacIntyre famously asked 'Is Patriotism a Virtue?' (1984). But perhaps the proper question is not whether patriotic loyalty is a virtue, but whether it is always a virtue. Here the answer is that it is not, since the ethical value of a person's attachment to the object of loyalty depends on whether that object is worthy of attachment. Patriotic loyalty is not virtuous when one's country's self-conception is necessarily warlike or racist. But this point can help us to see that patriotism *can* be a virtue, for even Nazi Germany's inherently aggressive and fascist character from 1933 to 1945 does not show that Germany was ever *necessarily* committed to hateful goals or that Germans cannot be good patriots. Before, during and after the Nazi period, many Germans expressed loyalty to their country by rejecting anti-Semitism, racism and war, opting instead for a patriotic understanding that calls on Germans to help their compatriots live up to noble ideals of responsible citizenship, human rights and international cooperation.

Patriotism, partiality and morality

Can a patriot be impartial?

Henry Louis Gates claims that loyalty is essentially a 'premodern virtue' because 'it bespeaks partiality', whereas our modern world demands impartiality, thereby sending loyalty into 'ethical exile'. But is Gates correct to interpret the requirement of impartiality as necessarily denying personal attachments to those near and dear to us? (Gates 1998: 36–7). A more promising suggestion is Samuel Scheffler's striking claim that loyalty and moral equality are both values that we must accommodate in our worldview, perhaps in irreconcilable tension with each other. They mutually constrain each other and compete in practice such that we must make difficult decisions about their relative priority. We recognize the appeal of love, loyalty and partial concern but also that of equality, respect for persons and impartial concern. It seems difficult to deny outright the relevance of either type of demand (Scheffler 2001: 79–81).

Two of the most prominent defenders of patriotism, Andrew Oldenquist and Alasdair MacIntyre, argue that patriotic concern cannot coexist with an impartial perspective that takes every person's interests equally into account. Oldenquist rejects as false what he labels 'impartial patriotism' (Oldenquist 1982: 183), while MacIntyre claims that patriots who appeal to 'impersonal' moral standards are actually holding an 'emasculated' patriotism to such an extent that it might not be real patriotism at all (MacIntyre 1984: 6). The basis of patriotic loyalty, according to MacIntyre, is that the country is *my* country, not that my country possesses some valuable or desirable characteristic such as natural beauty or satisfies some set of moral principles such as freedom and equality. If I am a patriot, my loyalty to my country is based on 'a particular historical relationship of association' between my country, its inhabitants, and me (4). If I were to discover that my country failed to live up to its self-professed moral ideals, I would not renounce that loyalty. In short, one can either be a true patriot whose loyalty depends on the facts of their own historical association, or be a false patriot whose attachment depends on the country's ability to meet a universalist test.

Both MacIntyre and Oldenquist seem to think that patriots who take universal morality seriously are in fact basing their patriotic attachment on universal criteria such as freedom, equality and human rights. But this misconceives the basis of patriotism as a species of loyalty. They fail to distinguish the particularistic psychological basis and emotional force of patriotism from the universal moral standards by which it should be evaluated (Nathanson 1993: 58–61). It is quite natural and common that we feel loyal to the country in which we were born or grew to maturity, and that we feel special affection for it and concern for its well-being. Patriotism does not originate or grow from a universal moral perspective; it is always a type of particular attachment. Yet loyalty to my country, while it must be loyalty to *my* country and not some other country if it is to count as patriotism, is like any other species of loyalty in being susceptible to moral assessment by reference to universal norms such as the demand to recognize others' (i.e., outsiders') basic interests or to avoid doing them harm.

Here it is relevant to mention Edmund Burke, whose *Reflections on the Revolution in France* (1790) was written in response to the Richard Price sermon we discussed in the Introduction. Burke claims that the vast majority of human beings possess natural sentiments – 'wisdom without reflection' – inclining them to love their own country because it is the country into which they were born and toward which they have been taught to be loyal (Burke 1982: 119). He believes it is necessarily the local that motivates us, so it is wrong to demand the impossible by appealing to love of humanity as the key moral motive (Bromwich 2014: 76–8). Burke's importance lies, then, not in his rejecting universal moral standards but in his affirming the particularity of moral motivation. The upshot is that concern for others must continue to focus on particular groups to which we belong – family, friends, country – rather than abstract humanity.

David Bromwich helpfully cites a persuasive response to this Burkean point. It comes from William Hazlitt's 1814 piece, 'On Patriotism – A Fragment', in which Hazlitt points out that modern patriotism is not produced by attachment to a localized community or homeland; instead it is 'the creature of reason and reflection' based on recognition of our country's abstract existence (Bromwich 2014: 85–6). As Hazlitt puts it, 'It is not possible that we should have an individual attachment to sixteen millions of men, any more than to sixty millions. We cannot be *habitually* attached to places we never saw, and people we never heard of. Is not the name of Englishman a general term, as well as that of man?' (cited in Bromwich 2014: 85). Consequently, both love of humanity and love of country are 'general affections' rather than forms of particularistic love, so it is false to imagine that patriotic particularity must take priority over morally universal concern for humanity.

What is impartiality?

Impartiality is widely thought to be at the core of moral thinking. Whether one takes morality to require us to produce the best overall consequences or to recognize universal basic rights and duties, the perspective we must adopt is judged to be an impartial one from which every person is entitled to equal consideration. From an impartial point of view, it does not matter whether someone is my compatriot. Especially when we are concerned with basic justice, the special relationships in which we participate are immaterial. The strong version of such a view, *first-order impartialism*, calls for each person to take up an impartial perspective in their own decision-making about what to do. The radical thinker William Godwin claimed that impartiality demands that we aim always to perform the action that is 'most conducive to the general good', allowing no fundamental role for any particular relationships in which we participate. So, he notoriously argues, if I can save only one of two people from a burning building – an archbishop whom we suppose will produce large social benefits through his writings, or a chambermaid who happens to be my mother – I should save the archbishop. What matters, says Godwin, is the amount of value a person is likely to produce, not whether she is my mother (or father or friend). 'What magic is there in the pronoun "my" to overturn the decisions of everlasting truth?' (Godwin 1971: 71).

First-order impartialism seems clearly mistaken because it requires us to show equal care and concern for everyone at all times in our decision-making while denying any role for friends, family, compatriots or personal pursuits in our deliberations. Even if this approach could rationalize special responsibilities by showing how they best promote the interests of everyone, it would leave out any possibility of recognizing the intrinsic value of relationships, like friendships, family ties and compatriot allegiances, that seem to form the core of worthwhile human lives. Consequently it seems reasonable to adopt a *second-order impartialism* that aims to assess from an unbiased, impartial perspective those relationships themselves, along with institutions like the nation-state or principles like freedom of association. The second-order view enables us to see, from an impartial perspective, why special relationships and loyalties are valuable and justified (Barry 1995: 217–33).

Human beings are not only objects of moral concern; we are also subjects with our own aims and interests (Wolf 2015: 33). Any adequate account of moral demands must accept this point, but it must also recognize the core idea that each of us is entitled to equal consideration: as deliberating agents we must somehow try to reconcile our own personal point of view with the impartial point of view. I see myself and my associates as central to my life's goals and plans, but I also acknowledge that I am not entitled to special privileges over any other person. This suggests a picture in which people may show special concern for those near and dear to them but must recognize the interests of distant and needy others with whom they have no particular association.

If patriotically partial relationships enable individuals to flourish by being part of a community whose members value the ties they all recognize, there is no reason why those relationships could not be condoned from a second-order impartial perspective. Compatriots should be restricted in what they may do to each other and to outsiders in the name of their country; but if these conditions are met, there seems to be a prima facie case for accepting compatriot partiality. Beyond this, the case could be made stronger by pointing out the potential for moral learning provided by solidaristic ties to fellow countrymen and countrywomen. We can learn to sympathize with the plight of outsiders by participating in the informal schools of family, friendships and compatriot relationships: care for the local needy can pave the way to care for persons generally.

So while recognizing the equal moral consideration demanded by impartiality, we can accept that patriotism is morally permitted. But this position seems to miss out a key point, namely, that patriotic special duties are *duties* rather than mere permissions. To see them as duties without deriving them from the bird's-eye perspective of impartiality, we must take them on their own terms, recognizing their value without authorizing them with the impartial stamp of approval. This suggests that patriots' associative duties are not derivable from the impartial point of view; nonetheless, these duties must acknowledge the impartialist demand that each person's interests count equally.

Does the impartial perspective exist?

While the impartial point of view seems to play an important role in moral thinking, Bernard Williams has offered two powerful objections to the very idea of impartiality. The first is that as a viewpoint it does not exist at all. According to Williams, 'the moral point of view is specially characterized by its impartiality and its indifference to any particular relations to particular persons', but this point of view is not one we can take up (Williams 1981: 2). Similarly, Iris Marion Young claims that 'the ideal of impartiality is an idealist fiction. It is impossible to adopt an unsituated point of view' (Young 1990: 104). To reason and act morally one must take up this perspective, but Williams and Young maintain that we are not capable of doing so: there are only the particular perspectives we adopt from our own personal points of view. So we cannot abstract from our own characteristics and commitments in order to decide what would be best for anyone considered as our moral equal. MacIntyre's defence of patriotism offers a critique of this kind. He sets the particularist morality of patriotism against a 'liberal morality' that 'requires of me to assume an abstract and artificial – perhaps even an impossible – stance, that of a rational being as such, responding to the requirements of morality not *qua* parent or farmer or quarterback, but *qua* rational agent who has abstracted him or herself from all social particularity'. This condemns me to being a rootless 'citizen of nowhere' (MacIntyre 1984: 12).

In response to what we can call Williams's and Young's (and MacIntyre's) nonexistence claim, it can be agreed that, in a literal sense, there is no objective and impartial viewpoint; there are only the many perspectives that each one of us possesses. But it is still possible for each of us to seek to understand that our own particular perspective is not morally privileged, that no one person is entitled to be valued above anyone else. This is all that is needed for impartiality to be both possible and desirable: it is the attempt to overcome personal bias and treat each person as an equal to every other. The outcome of impartial reasoning can be disputed, but it has not been shown that such reasoning is impossible.

The source of value: personal projects versus impartiality

Williams has another objection to make to impartiality. This one rejects the impartial perspective as a source of meaning and value for our lives, pointing instead to our individual 'ground projects' and commitments to play this role (Williams 1981: 12–13). We make sense of our lives through these personal projects and commitments as well as the attachments and relationships that often go along with them. Williams's second objection contains important truths, namely, that each of us has a life to live and that our personal commitments give our lives value. But from these facts it does not follow that impartiality should be rejected. On the contrary, while impartial norms do not give us special reasons to care for our personal projects or for our associates (family, friends, compatriots), nonetheless impartiality can and should count as a *constraint* on the pursuit of those projects. Williams's mistake is in thinking that impartiality, if it is to be defensible, must serve as the sole source of value in our lives. But if instead we view it as a normative check on our special relationships and projects, we can retain the truth in Williams's objection without rejecting impartiality as a core value. Patriotism can take a harmful form in which foreigners are disparaged and denied basic moral status, but other conceptions of patriotism are possible in which special responsibilities for one's compatriots are constrained by impartial concern for all human beings.

Conclusion

To sum up, we have claimed that patriotism involves accepting associative duties to one's compatriots. Three notions – community, loyalty and partiality – are prime candidates to justify these special responsibilities or duties to compatriots. Our community gives us our moral identities and provides roles for us to fulfil, but our moral agency requires that we decide for ourselves how to interpret the demands of those roles, including how strongly to emphasize love and loyalty to our country. We learn our values within communities, but this does not prevent us from considering ideas and arguments about value originating beyond them. To properly address moral disagreement and conflicts of loyalty, we must think for ourselves about the relative value of patriotism, friendship, family and other groups to which we belong. Patriotic loyalty to one's country involves perseverance in supporting it and a willingness to make sacrifices on its behalf, even at some cost to one's self-interest. But this loyalty is neither uncritical nor does it rule out judging one's country by appeal to universal moral values. Despite some prominent claims to the contrary, patriotic partiality is compatible with the demand to consider each person's interests impartially. Patriotism must be constrained by the requirement of equal consideration, but this demand cannot provide the basic reason for duties to sacrifice in the name of one's country. Even though impartiality is not the source of patriotism's ethical pull, it nonetheless aims to ensure that patriotic actions do not display undue bias by overlooking the legitimate claims of outsiders.

2
Nationalism, Patriotism and Cosmopolitanism

'National pride is to countries what self-respect is to individuals: a necessary condition for self-improvement.'
Richard Rorty (1998: 3)

'If you believe you are a citizen of the world, you are a citizen of nowhere.'
Theresa May, UK Prime Minister (quoted in Bearak 2016)

How is patriotism related to nationalism? Alasdair MacIntyre defines patriotism 'in terms of a kind of loyalty to a particular nation which only those possessing that particular nationality can exhibit' (MacIntyre 1984: 4). This exemplifies the practice of linking patriotic commitment to national membership, but is there a difference between national and patriotic forms of attachment? Sometimes it is claimed that patriotism is just another name for nationalism (Nathanson 1997: 178), but in John Kleinig's recent defence of patriotism, he distinguishes it from nationalism while at the same time identifying the characteristics to which patriotic commitment attaches – shared language, history, territory, culture and institutions (Kleinig et al. 2015: 27–8). These are some of the characteristics we would normally associate with national sentiments, so, since people often strongly identify with their nation and since both patriots and nationalists point to these common elements, it is worth focusing explicitly on nations and nationalism.

Nations play an important part in contemporary politics, from disputes over land and claims to secession to dilemmas about how to organize political institutions in light of people's collective identities. To understand why nations matter to people and whether there are good reasons to identify with one's nation, be loyal to it, and even be willing to die for it, we must first understand nations and nationalism.

Nations and nationalism

Why do people believe that they have special obligations to their compatriots? What is the social glue that binds them together? One prominent answer is *nationalism*, the idea that nations are groups of people whose members belong together and owe each other special obligations, including the obligation to govern themselves. David Miller's influential account says nations are historically continuous communities of belief with a sense of agency and mutual concern, tied to a particular territory, and with a shared public culture (Miller 1995: 22–7). Nations are communities whose members conceive of themselves as belonging to a group united by features such as language, history, ethnicity, culture, religion, territory and political institutions. Shared history is especially important from a normative perspective, given its capacity to be a focus for a person's sense of membership in the nation and a source of allegiance to her fellow nationals.

Nationalism comes in different varieties. Perhaps the key distinction in the present context is that between (1) an exclusivist, chauvinist nationalism that affirms the moral superiority of one's own nation over all others and legitimizes aggression against other nations, and (2) a liberal nationalism that recognizes the equality of persons, the rights of individuals to join together with others on the basis of shared cultural identity, and the equal claims of all nations to self-determination. Exclusivist nationalism falters on both empirical and moral grounds since its claim of superiority is bound to be false and, in any case, its moral rationalization of violence toward outsiders denies the legitimate claims of non-nationals to a fair hearing. We will therefore attempt to see what can be said for liberal nationalism.

Just as we distinguished country from state in Chapter 1, so we should now distinguish state from nation. A state is a territorially circumscribed political community that claims a monopoly of legitimate force within that territory (Weber 1946: 78), while a nation is a group whose members identify with each other and share an identity and solidarity based on some set of shared traits. So nations as identity-communities must be distinguished from states as territorial-political communities, yet nationalism links the two by emphasizing the desire of nations to be politically self-determining, which often will require the creation and maintenance of nation-states. Conceiving of co-citizens as co-nationals is a relatively recent historical development, having come to dominate political thinking and practice only since the late eighteenth century. The nation, or the people, became the focus of loyalty for everyone living within a given territory, replacing class- or status-based hierarchies with the egalitarian idea that everyone is fully a member of the nation. Within a particular state, the claim is that members of the national community share an identity, culture and language. The sense of shared national consciousness has been continuously created and re-created over the past few centuries by a process of state-generated nation-building involving the promotion of a national language and shared public culture through public education, a national news media, national holidays, flags and compulsory national service (Kymlicka 2002: 263). This sense of identity amongst a large group whose members cannot meet face to face – what Benedict Anderson (1991) calls an 'imagined community' – helps to promote the idea that a particular people is, say, Canadian or French or Italian. Nations tell themselves stories about their shared history: tales of victory and defeat that provide a sense of shared national agency, a common 'We' that acts in the world. Affirming one's national identity makes one a part of an intergenerational collective enterprise to which one can and should contribute.

As historically continuous communities, nations are 'communities of obligation' whose members must recognize the efforts of their forebears by acting in solidarity with co-nationals today to ensure the continuation of the community into the future (Miller 1995: 23–4, 2005: 68). Linda Colley famously argues that the modern British identity was forged out of English, Welsh and Scots elements by way of a shared majority commitment to Protestantism, parliamentary government and free trade, shaped during the eighteenth and nineteenth centuries in foreign wars and the growth of empire (Colley 1992). Being British meant not being French, but it also appealed to cultural markers like 'God Save the King' (1745) and the British Museum (1753). The continuing disputes about British identity – by groups representing workers, women, immigrant communities and constituent nations – include the questioning of its current constitutional framework and the rejection of its erstwhile imperial image (Miller 1995: 41, 166–72). Over time the dominant nation-constituting features may have changed, but the existence of a British nation crucially depends on its members believing themselves to belong to it. Ernest Renan's preferred metaphor for the nation is 'a daily plebiscite' in which its members affirm their 'agreement and clearly expressed desire to continue a life in common' (Renan 1939: 203). The 2016 'Brexit' referendum exemplifies how desires can change: small majorities in both England and Wales voted to leave the European Union, while slightly larger majorities in Northern Ireland and Scotland opted to remain. Given the potential implications of that vote, it is not surprising that the future of a common British identity remains uncertain.

It has become common to show solidarity with our fellow nationals, thereby thinking of the nation as itself an ethical community toward which we should show special concern and loyalty. National identity not only ties us to millions of others, near and far, within the boundaries of our nation-state; it also distinguishes us from foreigners who share among themselves a different national identity. Co-nationals share a sense of belonging to an historical community, tied to a particular territory, and advancing toward the future together. But is nationalism ethically defensible?

Nationalism: for and against

We will now consider some arguments for and against liberal nationalism as a normative account of political identity and obligations. Two themes stand out in support of nationalism: the role of nations in securing individual freedom and the need for national identity to provide the conditions for trust which in turn enable both democracy and social justice. And at least one sort of reason tells against nationalism: the so-called 'bad faith' objection that nationalists take part in a kind of self-deception that makes it difficult or impossible to know the truth about their nation.

Nationalism and freedom

The first argument says that national culture is a necessary condition for personal freedom or autonomy. If they are to make real choices about how to live their lives – that is, if they are to be autonomous – individuals need 'a range of meaningful options' from which to choose. The liberal nationalist claims that national culture provides these options as well as the depth of meaning needed for deciding among them. We should therefore recognize that individuals have a right to the protection of their national culture (Kymlicka 1995: 82–4). The main objection to this argument is that one can accept that access to culture is a precondition for individual autonomy without concluding that this culture must be national: human beings can live worthwhile lives in a range of cultural contexts, whether 'national, multinational, or non-national' (Stilz 2009: 141). If so, then the concern to protect and promote individual autonomy does not require a commitment to a single shared national culture. Consequently, a commitment to freedom does not support allegiance to the nation as a necessary condition for its promotion.

Nations, trust, democracy and justice

The second liberal nationalist argument is that shared nationality and its accompanying sentiments of solidarity are needed to achieve both democracy and social justice (Miller 1995: 162). The key role of national sentiment is to enable citizens to trust each other so that they can engage cooperatively in the give-and-take of democratic politics and be sufficiently motivated to support institutions of distributive justice. In fact, this argument also points to the role of national belonging as the implicit unifying force in any theory of liberal democracy (Tamir 1993: 117). In an age of ideological and religious fundamentalist division, an open and tolerant nationalism offers a unifying message that can bind people together in a common cause from which all may benefit. The underlying idea is that public spirit and social cooperation require that citizens (1) show restraint when democratic processes do not go their way, and (2) see their plight as shared with their compatriots. Both restraint and agreement to share one's fate with other citizens depend on *trust*, but (so the argument claims) trust is possible only when people share a national identity.

We saw in Chapter 1 that the mere fact of community membership cannot, by itself, provide a reason to accept obligations to fellow members. But the present claim is an empirical hypothesis about human motivation according to which nationhood is needed to produce amongst its members a willingness to trust each other and to make sacrifices for the common good (Stilz 2009: 148). But is this claim about motivation true? One reply to this argument is straightforward denial that shared national identity is necessary for democracy and social justice since, in fact, solidarity need not appeal to nationality. Consider multinational democracies, such as Canada and Switzerland, where relatively successful welfare states and democratic politics do not depend on a single, shared, cultural nationality. On the contrary, it seems that loyalty to one's own political community can provide the needed basis for trust without the appeal to cultural nationhood (Abizadeh 2002: 498).

A second reply to the argument denies, in a slightly different way, the claim that nationhood is needed to underpin social trust. Suppose it is true that the key to large-scale human social cooperation is our ability to create narratives in our collective imaginations. The problem, however, is that nationalist stories are not the only instance of this phenomenon: religious creation myths and the invention of money have also served the same purpose (Harari 2014: 25, 180). So the defence of nationality cannot be grounded in a claim about the nation's unique role in enabling trust and solidarity as the foundations of social cooperation.

Nationalism, history and truth

Alasdair MacIntyre points out that patriotism is not simply regard for one's nation because it is one's own; rather it includes regard 'for the particular characteristics and merits and achievements of one's own nation' as reasons for being patriotic (MacIntyre 1984: 4). As Richard Rorty suggests in the epigraph to this chapter, perhaps nationalists can engage in self-improving actions only if they are proud of their nation's achievements. Suppose, then, that patriotic loyalty refers to characteristics of one's nation and its history that are judged to be valuable. Simon Keller argues that this leads to bad faith, defined by Jean-Paul Sartre as 'hiding a displeasing truth or presenting as truth a pleasing untruth' (Keller 2005: 579). Bad faith is accepting, without good reason, beliefs that flatter one's nation and deceiving oneself about the source of those beliefs, likely leading to even further false beliefs (Keller 2007: 52–3). This is required to maintain a person's emotionally invested self-conception as a member of their nation. One does not typically choose the country toward which to be patriotic: often but not always the relevant country is the one into which one has been born. As young people are educated into the national culture, they are asked to accept views about their nation's history and characteristics aimed at eliciting emotional attachment and pride (Keller 2005: 581). The problem with this process of calling forth patriotic pride, according to Keller, is that it produces beliefs about one's country that must continue to be held even in the face of contrary evidence.

It is definitive of one common form of human irrationality to seek confirming evidence for one's beliefs while showing little or no interest in possibly disconfirming evidence. To form beliefs rationally, people should seek to refute hypotheses they are invited to believe, but instead they tend to 'seek data that are likely to be compatible with beliefs they currently hold' (Kahneman 2011: 81). This 'confirmation bias' is well known; it is instantiated in the context of nationalism with the additional force of *wanting* to have beliefs that reflect well on one's own nation. The incentive for nationalists to misunderstand their own history is an instance of 'motivated irrationality', namely, 'motivationally biased belief' in which individuals fail to follow generally reliable methods of evidence collection and evaluation (Mele 2004). National patriots, therefore, deceive themselves because they maintain a set of beliefs about their nation that is both irrationally held and necessary for continued patriotic commitment. In short, if one seeks to hold true beliefs about one's country, the result will be the inevitable recognition that the relevant valuable qualities are often absent. Love of country, on the other hand, threatens to give patriots an inaccurate picture of the world.

Nations are relatively modern inventions created in quite conscious ways by state action to produce a shared identity that would make social unity possible (Hobsbawm 1990). But does this aim jeopardize the pursuit of truth? To be clear, the objection is not that nations are unreal or totally imaginary; rather, the idea is that members of a nation have strong incentives to believe falsehoods and that these false beliefs can in turn lead them to misguided action. The logic of the bad faith objection is displayed clearly in the case of the state-supported teaching of history. If a central aim of education is to produce devotion to the homeland, there is a strong motive to shape historical narratives to achieve such devotion. We saw this at work in the Introduction when we considered the New York State *Manual of Patriotism*. The result can be a national history that is 'distorted, self-serving, and unselfcritical', rendering citizens insufficiently discerning in their assessment of the current government's policy and unconcerned with its effects on outsiders (Macedo 2011: 414).

Ernest Renan claimed that 'to forget and – I will venture to say – to get one's history wrong, are essential factors in the making of a nation; and thus the advance of historical studies is often a danger to nationality' (Renan 1939: 190). In his defence of the nation, David Miller interprets Renan to be saying that the point of forgetting events like religious massacres is not to deny the existence of such terrible acts but to deny that they 'form part of the story that the nation tells itself' (Miller 1995: 38). Nationalism is allegedly saved here by the nation recognizing the truth but distancing itself from the perpetrators of violence in its past. The problem, however, is that those who shape the narrative have a strong incentive to underplay and even distort such violence rather than focus on it and use it as a lesson about what not to do. An enlightened nationalism would include stories of heroism and tolerance but also truths about unjust treatment of religious or ethnic minorities. Yet it seems that real-world nationalisms tend to prove Renan's point that we hear the good and forget the unflattering parts of the story.

We should distinguish here between two possible conclusions: first, that nationalism *necessarily* leads to bad faith and false beliefs; second, that nationalism contains the *potential* to lead to these unattractive consequences. If the first conclusion is true, we have good reason to reject nationalism; but if the second conclusion is correct, we might want to be on our guard against the danger but still accept nationalism for its own intrinsic and instrumental value. To judge the relative merits of these two conclusions, let us consider the phenomenon of nation-building.

Nationalism tends to favour an overly unified picture of shared culture and language in a world that is in reality much more pluralistic both within and between nations. One of the lessons of nineteenth- and twentieth-century nation-building processes is to remind us how groups of people speaking countless local dialects were brought, through compulsory schooling, to speak the national language and identify with a particular national narrative (Weber 1976). But while nation-building produced social unity, it came with serious costs. First, those who resisted nation-building projects – indigenous peoples most obviously – were coercively, often violently, treated to ensure the imposition of the majority national identity. So nation-building has promoted solidarity amongst co-nationals often at the cost of war, colonialism and the attempt to wipe out group identities that would compete with the national narrative. Second, before the Second World War one central motive for states to engage in nation-building was 'to encourage uncritical patriotism, and the willingness to die for one's country' (Kymlicka 2002: 263–5). In other words, the dark side of nation-building includes its role in the tens of millions of war deaths during the first half of the twentieth century.

In recent decades, countries have started to come to terms with these great costs of nationalism through both clarifying the historical record and sometimes formally apologizing to the victims. This account of nation-building suggests, therefore, that it is possible to recognize past harms and acknowledge past wrongs while continuing to show allegiance to the nation as a continuously evolving intergenerational social project. A reply to Keller's bad faith critique, then, could point to national history as a source of both pride and shame. One of John Stuart Mill's causes of 'the feeling of nationality' is 'the possession of a national history, and consequent community of recollections; collective pride and humiliation, pleasure and regret, connected with the same incidents in the past' (Mill 1998: 427). Here we see the link between shared history and *both* 'pride and humiliation, pleasure and regret'. Fellow nationals, on this view, do and should concern themselves with the positive and negative sentiments generated by their shared historical narrative. Twenty-first-century German national identity might be a supporting example here, in so far as it stresses the evil of the Nazi period (1933–45) and the resulting sorrow and regret that must now be part of being German, along with a commitment to avoid any such shameful acts in the future. To be German today is to show concern for the truth about Nazi atrocities. Beyond facing up to the ugly elements in national histories, perhaps some of the sting can be taken out of the bad faith objection by affirming a conception of the nation as Renan's daily plebiscite in which members commit themselves to sharing a common life but with emphasis on the role played by contemporary political institutions, in which co-nationals are recognized as equals, rather than appealing to a national narrative whose moral pedigree is at best ambiguous.

Cosmopolitanism

The national community differs from the community of all human beings in size and, it seems, in moral and political relevance. Special obligations to compatriots ordinarily require people to pay taxes for social programmes like public education, health care and pensions that benefit only fellow citizens, while beyond one's country the demands are less burdensome. It is widely agreed that every person must avoid harming others regardless of location or citizenship status; many believe that each of us has a duty to contribute to securing access to clean water, food, shelter and basic health care for all human beings. But not harming others and ensuring minimal provision requires less from us than do the demands we recognize toward our compatriots. Does this show that we make use of a morally relevant distinction between co-nationals or compatriots on the one hand and outsiders on the other?

What is cosmopolitanism?

Cosmopolitanism is the idea that each person is a citizen of the world. It is directly opposed to the anti-cosmopolitan view of British Prime Minister Theresa May, quoted at the head of this chapter. In contemporary politics, the main cosmopolitan moral focus on the community of human beings contrasts with allegiance to the nation-state as a basic unit of concern. To see what cosmopolitanism implies about national or patriotic allegiance, we first must characterize cosmopolitanism itself in more detail. While we cannot provide an historical overview here (see Kleingeld and Brown 2013: part 1), we can say that when Diogenes the Cynic called himself a 'citizen of the world' in the fourth century BCE, he was rejecting any special claims that might be made on him by his local fellow citizens. Later developments in Stoic cosmopolitanism, through the European Enlightenment down to the present day, give more positive content to world citizenship and contain the core ideas that make up three types of cosmopolitan thought – moral, political and cultural – with a strong and a moderate version of each type.

Moral cosmopolitanism affirms the equal moral worth of each individual human being along with a universal commitment to take account of their interests without regard for any differences between them, including differences of nationality. In short, the community of human beings is the moral community to which we should pledge allegiance. Strong moral cosmopolitans defend duties to help others while denying any independent role for special relationships in justifying those duties, whereas moderate moral cosmopolitans argue that alongside duties to humanity we must acknowledge the non-derivative value of special relationships and the duties they entail (Scheffler 2001: 115). *Political* cosmopolitanism demands a greater role for coercive institutions beyond the currently dominant nation-state. Its strong variant argues for a world state and its moderate forms include advocacy of federal arrangements at the global level and international institutional frameworks addressing global problems such as climate change and war crimes. *Cultural* cosmopolitanism affirms the value of a multiplicity of cultures in enabling individuals to live good lives. In its strong form, it says that a good human life is possible only when persons have secure access to the goods of more than one culture, while the moderate form denies that persons can live a good life only if they are situated within one culture (Scheffler 2001: 116).

Our focus here is on moral cosmopolitanism, specifically on what can be said for it and what it implies about special responsibilities for co-nationals or compatriots. There is a range of arguments in support of cosmopolitan morality: utilitarians argue that the duty to maximize well-being should count everyone for one and no one for more than one; Kantians appeal to the universalizability of maxims on which we act and the requirement to treat humanity always as an end in itself; and proponents of human rights defend universal duties to ensure that each person's basic entitlements are met (Jones 1999: chapters 1–4). In each case, no appeal to nationality or citizenship is allowed to interfere with cosmopolitan equal consideration. Recent debates have focused on a core aspect of morality, namely the question of distributive justice: what is a just or fair distribution of the benefits and burdens of social cooperation? What do individuals have rights to and why? What is the role of nations in setting out the scope and demands of justice?

Cosmopolitanism, nationalism and patriotism

Cosmopolitanism about justice seems to imply that liberal nationalism fails to extend the reach of justice beyond nation-state borders to the community of all human beings. To limit justice to fellow nationals is to leave untouched the morally arbitrary fact that people's life prospects are largely determined by the country in which they happen to have been born. If, as some have argued (Beitz 1979: part 3), justice demands significant redistribution of income and resources across national borders through taxation, aid and trade that would benefit the globally worst-off individuals, national partiality appears to stand in the way of justice. In favouring our co-nationals, do we become numb to the legitimate interests of outsiders? Or can we love our nation 'as a project of collective self-rule in which the achievement of domestic justice is combined with due regard for the rights and interests of others with whom the world is shared'? (Callan 2006: 546). Defensible answers to these questions partly depend on assessing the relative merits of the strong and moderate moral cosmopolitan positions.

Consider first the strong view that recognizes at a basic moral level only our shared humanity and denies that bonds of nationality can be foundational premises in arguments about our rights. Patriotic concern is allowed only if it contributes to the universal good of humanity. Robert Goodin, for instance, argues that special duties to our compatriots are justified as an 'administrative device for discharging our general duties more efficiently' (Goodin 1988: 685). The goal is to fulfil our general duties to other human beings regardless of their nationality or citizenship; the means to achieve this goal is to use the efficiencies produced by the system of states, as long as each state possesses the capacity to contribute to the cosmopolitan goal. Without this instrumental connection, we seem to be forced to choose between (1) treating our compatriots as more important than outsiders, somehow limiting the scope of our primary concern to a subset of persons, and (2) treating every person as equally valuable, extending the scope of basic moral concern to all but leaving no room for compatriots at the foundational level (Scheffler 2001: 118). But moderate moral cosmopolitans accept as basic both general duties to all human beings and special duties to associates, including family, friends and compatriots. On this view, compatriot priority need not conflict with the demand to recognize the equal moral worth of every individual human being. We encountered this idea in the discussion of partiality in Chapter 1, but now we will consider a new argument, the so-called 'distributive objection', which applies to both strong and moderate cosmopolitanism and raises the spectre of injustice toward outsiders (Scheffler 2001: 56–64).

Are special duties to compatriots susceptible to the distributive objection? This objection points to allegedly excessive benefits that associative duties provide to compatriots, thereby disadvantaging outsiders. Members of the favoured national community do well by each other since their interests are protected by mutual recognition of duties to compatriots. But they do *unreasonably* well relative to others who do not benefit from the additional concern for in-group members that associative duties provide. Imagine an initially egalitarian distribution of duties between three people, followed by two of them joining a country together, thereby incurring associative duties to each other and reducing the claims on them of the third person who did not join. Even worse, their claims on him are as strong as before, so relative to them he is disadvantaged as both claimant and duty-bearer (Scheffler 2001: 56–7). In short, taking on compatriot-based associative duties can seem both anti-egalitarian and doubly harmful to the interests of outsiders.

For this reason among others, Scheffler claims to have identified a 'deep and persistent tension' between our special responsibilities or associative duties on the one hand and our general responsibilities on the other (Scheffler 2001: 109). But we need not settle on identifying this tension if it turns out that we obtain duties to non-compatriots by virtue of, rather than despite, our citizenship in political societies. This argument works by allowing the creation of groups to 'confer special advantages upon each other' if outsiders are free to do the same. But when outsiders are victims of their own states or when state collapse renders them in need of protection, citizens elsewhere have a duty to protect them and to help them build their own successful political societies (Vernon 2010: 104–5, 137–8).

Cosmopolitans point to the equal worth of each human being, regardless of nationality, as the basis for moral and political argument. If liberal nationalists defend principles of freedom and equality for their fellow nationals, cosmopolitans reply that every person possesses rights to be treated as free and equal by the institutions under which they live. The scope of moral and political concern, therefore, should not be limited to fellow nationals; instead it should extend to include everyone. When patriotic nationalists show special concern for their associates, they are simply imposing an arbitrary limit on the reach of ethical principles. Why should the fact that someone shares my nationality justify special treatment when outsiders possess the same moral value as fellow nationals? Liberal ideals of equal opportunity aim to overcome the effects of morally arbitrary features such as sex, gender, race and religion in determining life chances. But isn't national membership, which often stems from one's place of birth, just as morally arbitrary as these other characteristics? In all of these cases, we (mostly) do not choose the feature in question, so why should we arrange social institutions so that people do better or worse as a result of something for which they bear no responsibility? We owe respect and concern to every person without regard to the many differences between us, including national ones. It is certainly a fact that people now live in a world of nation-states, but there is no morally fundamental case for taking national membership to out-weigh the equal human rights possessed universally by every individual, regardless of the borders that happen to exist now.

Objections to cosmopolitanism

Cosmopolitanism can seem difficult to deny. After all, isn't it just a consistent attempt to interpret the 'egalitarian plateau' that any acceptable political theory must affirm, the idea that equal concern and respect are due to each individual person? (Kymlicka 2002: 3–4). Nonetheless, questions can be raised about its credibility and, if so, this may have implications for our understanding of nationalism and patriotism as well.

The first objection to cosmopolitanism is that it is a form of imperialism and, for that reason alone, must be rejected as a type of domination over the world's dispossessed peoples (Moore 2010: 141–2). The cosmopolitan perspective is an offshoot of the European Enlightenment, a movement whose claims to universal reason and freedom were belied by its association with colonial dispossession and aggression. Consequently, cosmopolitanism cannot achieve its desired universality because it will always be susceptible to the racist, sexist or other particularist commitments of its proponents. If true, this accusation would be severely damaging to the legitimacy of cosmopolitan moral theory and to the related campaigns to protect and promote human rights globally. But two points can be made in reply. First, as Sankar Muthu (2003) has shown, Enlightenment cosmopolitanism contained many powerful voices against colonialism and imperialism, including that of Immanuel Kant, so cosmopolitan thinking is separable from imperialism. Second, any version of this imperialism objection is best dealt with by sticking yet more consistently to the cosmopolitan moral demand to treat all persons as moral equals, to show equal concern and respect for persons regardless of nationality, culture, religion, sex, gender, race or wealth. This demand is fundamentally incompatible with imperialism and domination.

A second objection to cosmopolitanism is the charge that it is psychologically unrealistic because it makes an impossible demand that we should be motivated to care about a massive yet abstract community like humanity. Equal moral concern for everyone is 'too diluted to be able to generate effective moral enthusiasm and too weak to outweigh narrower loyalties' (Oldenquist 1982: 181). The point here is that the cosmopolitan's impartial perspective demands equal concern for all persons but, since we are incapable of summoning the motivation to meet this demand, our loyalties will remain inevitably focused on family, friends and country. We simply cannot show concern for humanity as a group: there are too many people, we are not directly connected to enough of them, and our imaginations are such that we necessarily gravitate to smaller identity communities. In reply to these charges, cosmopolitans must recognize that appeals to our shared humanity do not stand out as the most effective motivating calls to action. Yet the critic overlooks the fact that we *can* be moved by recognizing our shared humanity (Glover 1999: 22–30): consider not only the response we make to victims of natural disasters or war-ravaged suffering in far-off places but the heroic acts of many 'righteous *goyim*' who, at great risk to their own lives, saved Jews during the Holocaust

(Nussbaum 1996: 131–2, 143–4). Moreover, whether we are pulled toward co-nationals more strongly than others is, in part, the result of a socialization process which is subject to revision, at least to some extent, in accordance with the whole range of our moral responses.

Constitutional patriotism

If nationalists tie political allegiance to national culture and cosmopolitans declare their commitment, at a fundamental level, to all human beings, for constitutional patriots 'political attachment ought to center on the norms, the values and, more indirectly, the procedures of a liberal democratic constitution' (Müller 2007: 1). This can be seen as a kind of middle ground between nationalism and cosmopolitanism since constitutional patriotism, like nationalism, aims to justify a particularist attachment but does so, like cosmopolitanism, by appealing to universal values. The idea originated in post-war West Germany and, as developed by Jürgen Habermas (1994), came to be understood as attaching loyalty to constitutional principles rather than shared nationality.

For Habermas, citizenship means not only political membership but equal status defined by civil rights. For co-citizens, shared national culture is neither necessary nor appropriate as a focus of collective allegiance; rather, what is needed is shared 'political culture' that serves as 'the common denominator for a constitutional patriotism' that at the same time enables the persistence of a stable, liberal-democratic, modern, multicultural society. Habermas wants to ensure that attachments to our fellow citizens can provide 'particularist anchoring' while preserving 'the universalist meaning of popular sovereignty and human rights' (Habermas 1994: 25, 27–8).

One hope for constitutional patriotism is that it could enable fellow citizens to share a commitment to liberal-democratic constitutional values as a way of identifying with their country. But it has been argued that this has not been the case (Kymlicka 2003: 378–80). Consider attempts to foster a pan-Canadian identity that would be shared by Canada's constituent English, French and Indigenous nations. In recent decades, political values amongst these communities converged on a set of civil, political and social rights, but at the same time more Quebeckers identified as 'Québécois' than 'Canadian'. It seems that shared values cannot substitute for shared identity.

Habermas's constitutional patriotism has been accused of being bloodless as well as too abstract and formalistic to be able to provide the energy to bind a people culturally to each other (Canovan 1996: 87–97; Kleinig et al. 2015: 42). But there might be a persuasive argument that constitutional patriotism can be conceived not merely as commitment to universal political principles but as a particular democratic project that co-citizens value for the form it takes in their own country. If so, there might be a way to link patriotic commitment not only to universal constitutional principles but to the democratic process itself, so that co-citizens value their shared role in 'collective democratic participation' and show 'loyalty to a particular project of democratic citizenship' (Stilz 2009: 153–4, 160). These thoughts lead us in new directions that we will now address in Chapter 3.

3
The Republican Alternative

'Every patriot hates foreigners, for to him they are only men.'
Jean-Jacques Rousseau (1911: 7)

'When we consider how ardent a sentiment ... the love of country has become, we cannot judge it impossible that the love of that larger country, the world, may be nursed into similar strength.'
J. S. Mill (1884: 107)

It is sometimes held that patriotism necessarily tends to converge with nationalism, for a patriot is likely to admire and identify with features of the culture and history of her country, and shared culture and history, as we have seen, are just the features that are pointed to as constitutive of national identity and attachment (Kleinig et al. 2015: 40–1). But sometimes the connection between the two ideas is emphatically or even vehemently denied, most notably by Maurizio Viroli in his book *For Love of Country* (1995). According to Viroli, nationalism is to be seen as a comparatively recent political idea, one deriving largely from nineteenth-century Romantic beliefs about the importance of ethnicity and local culture to peoples' identity, beliefs arising from resistance to the cosmopolitan values of the European Enlightenment. Rejecting cosmopolitanism, and focusing upon what is distinctive to each society, nationalists, Viroli claims, tend strongly toward exclusiveness, or even, at the extreme, toward lending their support to hostility to outsiders. Because of the great influence of nationalism in the past two centuries, the older tradition of patriotism often comes to be seen as sharing in its exclusive tendencies. But in fact, he continues, patriotism should properly be seen as a political belief in the fundamental value of free political institutions and of the importance of active, engaged citizenship in supporting freedom; that is, as an idea belonging to the *republican* tradition, a tradition that gives a central place to self-government. That is an inclusive ideal, not one that lends itself to hostility among peoples. In stressing inclusiveness, Viroli's version of patriotism inherits a long tradition of political thought, from eighteenth-century writers such as Richard Price, whom we discussed in the Introduction, to contemporary theorists who see patriotism as a radical ideal committed to advancing the republican idea worldwide. (See Varouxakis 2006 for a particularly illuminating historical survey.)

Some selectiveness may be necessary in claiming the term 'patriotism' for this tradition uniquely. We must, for example, overlook Rousseau's notorious remark, quoted at the head of this chapter, expressing a view that would make (republican) patriotism as radically exclusive as nationalism is said to be. The idea that the usage of the terms patriotism and nationalism can be separated as cleanly as Viroli proposed has been much questioned. But his proposal has the great merit of isolating another important basis for patriotism that takes that idea in a distinctive direction. In this chapter we assess its potential and its limits.

Between civic humanism and liberalism

In focusing on valued political relationships in this way, republicans often feel the need to distinguish their position from another similar-looking one, termed 'civic humanism'. Whereas republicans trace their lineage to Machiavelli and his successors, and, through Machiavelli, to the example of the Roman republic, civic humanism is commonly traced to Aristotle and the values of the Greek city-states. In his famous statement, in Book I of the *Politics*, that 'Man is a political animal', Aristotle epitomized the view that it was only in active participation in the affairs of the city that human nature could achieve its self-perfection. Only in civic participation could the distinctively human powers be developed. Notoriously, this has always been a highly selective ideal, both in the sense that it could only be achieved in certain kinds of society (Greek cities) and in the sense that even within those societies only certain kinds of people (adequately wealthy men) could attain it. Given the range of ideals and values on offer in modern pluralist societies the Aristotelian ideal would be at best only an optional one, and attempts to recover it in some form tend to meet with accusations of other-worldly remoteness (Honohan 2002: 131). So it is understandable that republicans should need to put some distance between their own 'neo-Roman' conception and a 'neo-Greek' view, as we may call it, with marginal political traction today, thus escaping the charge of utopianism.

In distancing republicanism from civic humanism, an important distinction is made between the intrinsic and the instrumental valuing of political participation. It is of course open to anyone to adopt an engaged political life as a personal ideal, just as they may adopt religious or familial or aesthetic personal ideals. For such people, republicanism would be a personal ideal as well as a political value. But the political value does not rest on anyone's personal endorsement. The political value lies in the fact that personal liberties are secure only if there is general involvement on the part of the public as a whole in the conduct of civic life. The historian Quentin Skinner develops this line of thinking in several influential books (see especially Skinner 1998). Only in a polity with an active, engaged, critical public can freedom be created and preserved. Political engagement doesn't define the meaning of life, but it protects us from tyranny.

As a result of this, however, republicans need to watch their border with another political conception, liberalism. For liberals too of course value liberties and advocate political institutions that will protect them. But republicans often present themselves as offering a better alternative to what they regard as a dominant liberal consensus in political thought, and this claim depends on their showing that what they offer is importantly distinctive. Their claim leans heavily on an idea that in the early modern literature is called enslavement, and in contemporary writing is called domination (Pettit 1997: chapter 2). This idea depends in turn on a particular way of thinking about freedom, in terms of vulnerability to the decisions of others. You are unfree (enslaved, dominated) if another is in a position of power over you such that, at their discretion, they could deny you the freedom to act. In a famous phrase in *Leviathan*, Hobbes wrote that 'A freeman is he that, in those things which by his strength and wit he is able to do, is not hindered to do what he has a will to' (Hobbes 1994: 136). But on the non-domination view, the person is free only if another is in no position to hinder him at *his* will. It is not hindrance to my will, but exposure to another's, that makes me unfree.

This view incorporates, rather than rejecting, the idea of freedom as non-interference, or as not being hindered or obstructed. Skinner does not wholly depart from that idea. As he points out, the neo-Roman view that he presents and defends is different from the original Roman view in incorporating an idea of rights (Skinner 1998: 18–21). Early modern political thought was deeply coloured by the idea of natural rights, an idea with no clear Roman or other classical precursor, and the republican writers of the seventeenth century built into their political theory the claim that such rights could only be sustained by means of the system they favoured. The civic engagement that they valued was important exactly because it was essential to the protection of civil and political liberties, which will inevitably be lost if citizens fail to be watchful. Replying to the complaint that he has offered no reason to differentiate the republican view from the liberal view, Skinner relies heavily on that claim: while republicans and liberals may believe in the same rights, only the republicans provide an account of the political conditions needed to sustain them over time (84n).

We need to distinguish between what may be termed conceptual and causal versions of Skinner's idea of enslavement. On the conceptual view, you simply are unfree if an opportunity is not open to you, whether you are aware of or desire that opportunity or not. So, to borrow an example from Locke's *Essay Concerning Human Understanding*, if I am locked in a room but have no desire to leave it, being happily engaged in pleasant activities that I find entirely absorbing, I am unfree nevertheless (Locke 1975: 238). We are to measure freedom or unfreedom in terms of possible desires (or perhaps worthwhile possible desires), and not only in terms of the preferences that people currently have. That interpretation leads in interesting but politically indeterminate directions, involving as it does essentially open-ended speculation about what people would want if they did not want what they do want. There may well be an important place for specula-tion of that kind. Perhaps, in order to assess whether or not people are free, we need to make evaluative judgements about what kinds of actions are potentially important for them, and not just take their actual preferences as given (Taylor 1991). But Skinner does not go down that road, sometimes called the 'positive freedom' road, which might well lead, in this case, in a civic humanist direction – for he grasps the other alternative, that of examining the causal effects of domination on our actions. When we are dominated, we foresee the consequences of disobedience or heterodoxy, and so we change our behaviour in anticipation. The problem is general, but it applies with especial force, he points out, to those citizens with a particular duty to speak truth to power, ministers and advisers. As ample evidence suggests, they will fail in that duty once they know that unwelcome truths will be punished, and so they are unfree to utter those truths even if they do not actually utter them and get to be punished for doing so.

Two general issues are raised by the republican or neo-Roman defence of patriotism. One is whether, as its advo-cates such as Skinner claim, it is different enough from more familiar liberal ideas to count as very distinctive. The claim to distinctiveness is resisted on the grounds that it ascribes too simple or Hobbesian an idea of freedom to liberalism (Patten 1996), or unduly homogenizes the liberal tradition (Isaac 1988), or that liberal freedom is normatively prior to repub-lican freedom (De Bruin 2009). The causal version of the domination thesis – i.e., power need not be used when its use is anticipated – has long been familiar to political scientists and political actors. But that issue, whatever its importance in other contexts, can be left aside here. The second issue, however, is crucial to the defence of patriotism. It brings into play a basic distinction made in Chapter 1 above. The republican idea of civic engagement is – like liberalism in this respect at least – a universal one, not one confined to people with a particular ethnicity or culture. We are to value our republic, and engage in its political life, because it embodies a political good, the good of non-domination. But why should we value that good, and pursue it, only *here*, or here more particularly than in some other place?

In 1936, a democratically elected government in Spain was opposed by a military insurrection supported by the fascist governments in Germany and Italy. Some 30,000 volunteers, from, it was claimed, more than fifty countries, came to Spain to fight for the 'Republican' side, as it was called, despite the neutrality or outright opposition of their own countries. It was obviously their view that, if democratic self-government was a basic political value, then it should be defended where it most needed defence, or where its defence was crucial. In cases such as this, the universal ideal and the particular attachment that it is meant to sustain come apart. Can they be put together?

Republican particularity

Viroli insists that the liberty that republican citizens want to defend is 'their own'. Their love of country, as we have seen, is not a love bounded by cultural, ethnic or religious identity. It is, rather, a love of 'common liberty': the 'common liberty of a particular people, sustained by institutions that have a particular history which has for that people a particular meaning, or meanings, that inspire and are in turn sustained by a particular way of life and culture'. He continues: 'I do not mean love of the republic in general or attachment to an impersonal republic based on universal values of liberty and justice. I mean the attachment to a particular republic with its particular way of living in freedom' (Viroli 1995: 12–13). The thought here is evidently complex. As we have seen, the tradition in which it seems natural to locate Viroli's book is one that *could* be said to rest on 'universal values of liberty and justice', a tradition that, for example, led British Radicals such as Price to endorse American and then French liberty, in the face of the policies and self-identified interests of their own country. Analogies between one country's liberty and another's are common, and vivid. The 'Va pensiero' chorus from Verdi's opera *Nabucco*, a lament for the ancient captivity of Hebrew slaves, was intended to resonate with rising Italian nationalism in the mid nineteenth century, and in fact still functions today as an unofficial Italian national anthem. The cover of Viroli's own book portrays an image from Greek history – painted by the French artist Delacroix – that is obviously meant to have transnational meaning. So in what sense does the patriot 'not' love a 'republic in general', but a particular one?

It is of course true in a trivial way that it is one's own liberty that one experiences rather than someone else's, in the same sense in which one wears one's own shoes, not someone else's. But nothing would follow from that. The point must be that one's liberty is distinctive in some way other than being the one that's experienced, that it has something distinctive in its content. And that is surely true. When nineteenth-century Italian nationalists saw analogies between their own plight and that of the enslaved Hebrews, surely they knew that suffering interference by European powers was not quite the same as being put to hard labour in Egypt. They evidently thought, though, that what they had in common was, in context, significant enough that the disanalogies didn't need to be mentioned. Conversely, when people think directly about their own traditions of liberty, they may well focus on local traditions that, as Viroli says, have a particular history and meaning behind them. In Britain, for example, the Westminster tradition of constitutional democracy is full of colourful and arcane myths and practices to which British patriots may feel attached. But despite this, surely it is the principle of democracy that, in the last resort, they would fight for, rather than, say, the practice of symbolically compelling the Speaker of the House of Commons to take his seat (a practice recalling the violent early history of Parliament, when taking on the role of Speaker could be lethal). Why insist that it is the local practice, rather than the principle mediately reflected in it, that is the object of love?

That question remains even if we take a still more forceful story about identification, one that turns on the importance of shame and honour. Such a version is offered by Charles Taylor in his account of why it is crucial that patriotism involves 'a *particular* common enterprise', or 'common allegiance to a particular historical community' (Taylor 1989: 166, 176). Taylor employs the example of political scandals, such as Watergate in Nixon's administration in the United States, and points out quite rightly that those American citizens who were appalled by it reacted much more 'vigorously' (174) than they did to abuses of power – much more violent and serious ones – in other countries in that period. They felt, in other words, that it was not just a principle that had been violated, but that *their* principles had been violated. There was, he says, a widespread identification with an American way of life defined by ideals and enshrined in famous documents, and it was this 'pride and attachment' that explains why people were outraged by 'the shady doings of a Watergate' (174). The argument for patriotism, then, is that it is only when one's sense of pride is locally engaged that one will respond to abuse with the vigour that the defence of good institutions requires. Defending good institutions is possible only when there is 'a love of the particular' rather than an endorsement of abstract principle (176). This is an important argument, given that there is evidence for the role that feelings such as shame and honour play in sustaining and changing shared moral convictions. In a different context, Kwame Anthony Appiah (2010) has shown, taking several interesting historical examples, how what he terms 'the honour code' moves people to take a stand against abuse in a way that abstract principles generally fail to do. But that cannot be a free-standing explanation. We feel shame about things that we believe to be shameful, and take pride in things that we believe to be worthy. It is true that those things must be 'ours', but that they are ours cannot, on its own, explain their moral force. We must also feel that whether we protect or abandon them is enormously consequential. When a US president authorizes burglary, that is consequential. If a US president were to overlook the tradition of pardoning a turkey at Thanksgiving, or throwing out the first pitch of the baseball season, it would not be, even if those traditions had attained 'way of life' status, as, plausibly, they have. We are back to the importance of what is at stake.

If we were to say, however, that what is at stake is not a principle but the bare fact that something is distinctively ours, something that other societies do not have, that would take us directly back to the nationalist view, from which, it seems, the republican view was to be clearly separated. We would be supposed to be deeply embedded in a particular historically constructed and culturally supported way of doing things; and if that were the primary fact about us and our motivation, we would have to conclude that it was merely a fortunate fact that our own way of doing things just happened to include institutions that promoted political freedom. We would be on exactly the same plane, in terms of political morality, as citizens of other states whose deep attachments to traditional ways of doing things happened, sadly, to consign them to domination and passive acquiescence. If we want to resist that conclusion, by giving primacy to the attachment to liberty – whatever its locally idiosyncratic embodiment happens to be – then we are back to endorsing a universal value.

Now we could of course say that Viroli's rejection of 'general' republicanism related simply to the question of motivation. We do not, as a matter of fact, first come to love the 'general republic' and then arrive at love of our own, as a nearby exemplar of it. We first love our own, and only then can it happen that our love 'extends beyond national boundaries and translates into [transnational] solidarity' (Viroli 1995: 12) – a claim to be critically considered below. But even so, if it is the potential extension of the love that makes it morally admirable, then it is its extension, not its initial motivation, that makes it justifiable. To refer again to William Godwin's famous thought-experiment, the motivation to rescue one's own spouse, rather than a stranger, from a fire is a feeling that is easily justified. The motivation to rescue one's own stock certificates, rather than a helpless stranger, is not. There are worthy and unworthy motives, and they do not carry their justification within themselves. As we saw, Godwin asked, rhetorically, why it is that people suppose there to be magic in the pronoun 'my' (Godwin 1971: 71). Surely if there is any 'magic', it would come from the conjunction of the possessive pronoun with some, but not other, accompanying nouns.

Republican universalism?

The best defence of the moral necessity of republican patriotism comes from what may be a surprising place; namely, Pauline Kleingeld's account of 'Kantian Patriotism' (2000) – perhaps surprising, because Kantian views are frequently seen as hostile to any version of moral or political particularity, being fundamentally universalist in nature. Kantian ethics tells us that we should will only what can be universally willed, not what some subset of people can will to their own benefit. But Kleingeld nevertheless makes, within a Kantian framework, a compelling case for one kind of patriotism. She calls it 'civic patriotism', but it is located clearly within the republican tradition, in that the object of patriotic attachment is a self-governing political society. She distinguishes republican or civic patriotism from two other kinds: nationalist and trait-based. The nationalist version of patriotism, as we have seen, draws on shared history or ancestry or culture or language or several of these. Trait-based patriotism is based on pride in some feature of one's country, such as its physical beauty, its music, its elegant lifestyle, and so on. In Kleingeld's civic patriotism, '[t]he republican state ... is regarded as serving the common good of the citizens in the political sense. The citizens are regarded as free and equal ... individuals who are united in their pursuit of a common political good.' Their love of this freedom 'manifests itself in civic activity ... whether this takes the form of governing it, defending it, or promoting the well-being of its citizens' (Kleingeld 2000: 317). But can this be not just a love, but a duty? Kleingeld believes that it is a duty, and her argument takes two major steps. First, drawing upon Kant, it is claimed that there is a duty to create just institutions to regulate the freedom of persons who interact with one another (324–5). Second, drawing upon the causal analyses made familiar in the republican tradition, it is claimed that just institutions of the appropriate kind – democratic states – can work and survive only if citizens play an active role (327). That claim, Kleingeld continues, *determines* the kind of relationship that is necessary between citizen and state, so that 'a duty to promote just states *without* a duty of civic patriotism is incoherent' (329).

This position is to be distinguished from a similar-looking case, also Kantian in inspiration, the 'ethical patriotism' advocated by Marcia Baron (1989). Similar freedom- and democracy-promoting themes appear in that position, which maintains, simply put, that patriotic attachment to one's country is justified as long as one's country affirms and advances those values, internally and in its external relations. Such a view would belong, applying Kleingeld's typology, to the 'trait-based' class of patriotisms: we value our country because it has good features. As a member of that class of patriotisms, it is open to the objection that if one's loyalty is to the trait, then one should lend one's support either to the country that best exemplifies it, or, alternatively, to the country most in need of it, and not to one's own unless it just happens to meet one or other of those conditions.

Kleingeld's view is distinctive, too, in denying that there are special duties *to co-citizens*, as opposed to a duty to promote a particular kind of political order (Kleingeld 2000: 332). This circumvents the large and contested issue, outlined in Chapter 1 above, regarding the justification of partiality. What principle allows us to give special treatment to people with whom we associate? One proposed answer, as we saw, takes a route through the intrinsic value of (some kinds of) associative relationship. When we confer a benefit on an associate, we express not only the good of conferring that benefit but also the value of that relationship, so that, to revert to the time-honoured example, when we rescue a spouse from a fire we simultaneously perform a universally good act (rescuing from danger) and affirm the value of a particular relationship (our marriage). Now if citizenship is, like marriage, intrinsically valuable, we can say that, similarly, giving preferential treatment to co-citizens has such a double aspect, which distinguishes it from giving a comparable good to a stranger, which has one aspect only (Mason 1997). Suppose we agree that shared citizenship can be seen as an associative good that we affirm in the way in which we treat other citizens. A problem of priority remains. There are many other associative goods, some within and some beyond a country's borders. For Antigone, in Sophocles' play, the associative good of siblinghood trumped the associative good of being Theban. For nuclear physicists in the 1930s the associative good of their global community came into a tense relationship with the associative good of their various nationalities. There seems to be a general impossibility in laying down a stable or across-the-board hierarchy of associative goods, as we would have to in showing that patriotism could be a duty. Here Kleingeld's solution is free of that difficulty. It gets free of it, however, by implicitly requiring us to abandon one part of the standard definition of patriotism, that is, that it should entail special regard for compatriots; but that part of the definition (to be discussed further in the following chapter) may be dispensable, and in any event this Kantian version of patriotism effectively continues to allot special *treatment* to compatriots, even though that treatment is not based on special regard for them, but is mediated through an institutional loyalty.

We can say, then, that Kantian patriotism is a partial success in grounding a republican approach. Is it enough of a success? A question mark may remain over the kind of 'support' that we can be said to have a duty to give. The argument is that since a democratic republic cannot survive without engaged citizens, then every citizen has a duty to become politically engaged. There may be some slippage here between engagement and political engagement. For there are forms of engagement other than political ones that are no less essential to the survival of democratic societies. Engagement in teaching is one example: 'so long as a single one vegetates uneducated', the Italian patriot Mazzini wrote, 'you have not got a Country such as it ought to be' (quoted in Viroli 1995: 149). If it is true that democracy depends on a certain level of wealth creation, then engagement in that would be another example. If just (defensive) wars are permitted, then engagement in developing military skills would be another. The teacher, the entrepreneur and the soldier might all have a strictly professional attitude to their callings, and whether patriotism (of any kind) enters into their attitude would seem to be a strictly optional matter. Rousseau himself suggested something like this when, in his *Discourse on Political Economy*, he complained that one may be an excellent priest or soldier or businessperson but a bad citizen (Rousseau 1987: 115), without however saying anything to resolve the question at hand: can patriotism be a generally required value when other values are also essential to the flourishing of political communities?

Beyond the republic

The final question to be addressed here is a comparative one, that is, a question about the strength or scope of republican duty in relation to other duties. It would, of course, be only a paper duty if it were to turn out that, while there was a case for it, other more urgent duties left no real space for it to operate. Kantian patriotism does not, course, deny the existence of other duties. They set 'clear constraints' on what civic patriotism can require of us – 'I should not procure the means for discharging my civic duty by deceiving others or by violating their right to freedom' (Kleingeld 2000: 333), a condition that we take to apply to the case of those outside one's *patria* as well as those within it. That evidently leaves quite a space to be filled in: short of violating others' freedom, there are areas of action in which devoting resources to one's own society cannot but deny those resources to another. In his famous essay, Alasdair MacIntyre, as we saw, took the view that such conflicts are pretty well endemic, citing historical cases in which societies with different economic needs necessarily come to blows over competing uses of land. That view may beg the question by simply assuming that, before the claims are staked, the countries concerned are unconstrained by considerations of justice, that they can take their own needs to be sovereign. Many republicans, including and especially Kantian ones, would dispute this. But does the republican tradition point us toward moral limits on external claims, and, if so, how much space is left for patriotic attachments? Here are some constructive proposals that have been offered.

Republican human rights

There are of course many ways of grounding the idea of human rights and of defining their content and scope (Cruft et al. 2015). But republicans should be attracted by certain approaches to this issue. First, of course, they would need to endorse those ideas of political rights that they share with liberalism: rights to express oneself, to associate with others, and not to be excluded from full civic status on arbitrary grounds. They would endorse these 'liberal' rights from their own perspective, that is, they would endorse them as necessary conditions for civic participation. But their idea of rights would need to extend further, whatever it is that liberals may conclude from their own point of view. While recognizing the importance of distinctive political contexts, they would need to endorse human rights that protected people from any form of coercion that impeded their civic participation (Ivison 2010). So, at a maximum, they may have to deny legitimacy to any regime that practises systematic exclusion on arbitrary grounds such as gender or ethnicity. That denial could amount to refusing to accept the regime's participation in international institutions, or to a refusal to accept it as a trading partner, for example. At a minimum, it would amount to a refusal to become directly complicit in repression in other countries; for example, by selling arms that enable legitimate opposition to be physically crushed.

Global non-domination

In addition to the question of complicity in aiding internal domination in other countries, there is the issue of the direct domination of one country by another. Of course it is well known that strong countries can, if they decide to, extract favourable terms of association from weaker ones. But we miss a great deal of what is going on if we focus only on coercive situations, while leaving aside the situations in which it is the anticipation of a coercive response that leads poorer countries to come to disadvantageous terms with more potent partners. If that were not so, we could make no sense of the idea of exploitation in cases in which both parties to a deal voluntarily sign up to it, despite the fact that the consequences of not signing are far more serious for one party than for the other (Sample 2003). Here the republican idea of non-domination shows its great value. It is not (only) what you are doing to me now, but what I know you could do to me if and when you decide to, that determines the question of my freedom.

Global institutional requirements

It was argued above that the most compelling version of republican patriotism drew upon Kant's idea that if persons are in interaction, in ways that affect the use of their freedom, then they have a duty to create an institution that will regulate their interactions fairly. He had in mind, of course, the creation of a state. But when states in turn interact, the same institution-creating logic would seem to apply no less well. There are, of course, international institutions that states accept as bodies that constrain their economic interactions. But they do not give equal status to states in the way in which states, on the republican ideal, give equal weight to their own citizens. A committed republican, then, would see the moral necessity of correcting the unequal representation of states in the international bodies that oversee the terms of economic interaction among them. Moreover, a republican who was alive to all forms of domination would also demand a response to those that circumvent states altogether, that is, the exposure of populations to the unaccountable power of corporations that have achieved virtual immunity from control by either their home countries or the countries in which they operate (Laborde 2010).

A possible objection, open to republicans who resist moderating their patriotism in that way, is that only states have the resources necessary to counter domination. Quoting several republican authors, Frank Lovett explains this as the view that the rule of law is the only institutional means to prevent domination by compelling citizens to observe 'relational equality' in their arrangements. Only a coercive institution can do this, and perhaps it is also the case that 'shared norms and standards' are so country-specific that the enforcing agency must be a local one (Lovett 2016: 38). Republicans who hold such views will recognize a transnational duty of assistance, that is, a duty on the part of wealthier societies to transfer to poorer ones resources enabling them to establish their own local political freedom. But that duty is less demanding than the duty on the part of compatriots to promote social and economic equality among themselves in order to remove the sources of domination. So compatriots come first, on this view, despite some significant transnational obligations: what is owed them is not just a threshold amount, but an ongoing requirement of egalitarian justice. Lovett's objection to the view involves a switch of perspective from what a republic owes to other polities to considerations about what a republican should believe is owed to (all) individuals (42; see also Pettit 2016). Inequality and poverty make people subject not only to oppression by states and injustice at the hands of international institutions and regimes in which their voices are not fairly represented, but also to exploitation by non-state actors. Lovett considers several practical conclusions that he believes republicans should draw from this (44–6), and to his list one might add another, that is, the effort by international lawyers to provide states with the legal means to hold corporations within their territories accountable for their actions elsewhere, in countries with populations whose lack of opportunity makes them vulnerable to exploitation (Seck 2013).

Transnational republican community

A still stronger departure from a purely patriotic ideal is suggested by James Bohman's 'Republican Cosmopolitanism' (2004). It is a feature of the global political economy today that its impacts reach 'indefinite others', that is, they are serious but diffuse. Just because they are diffuse, they will not have received the consent of all those whom they affect, who in that sense are dominated even though we cannot (always) point to a dominator standing in a specific relation to them (as in the simpler case of a tyrant, for example). It follows that the appropriate response to such domination must be open to constant renegotiation (Bohman 2004: 339–40), and such responses cannot plausibly be contained within national political structures. 'Transnational publics' (347) may be required for accountability to be established, and creating and supporting such publics would of course amount to a significant departure from patriotism.

Honorific republicanism

On the above arguments, then, a republican – for the very same reasons that sustained her republican patriotism – would have to accept limits to what could rightfully be devoted to her own *patria*, for all of the above proposals entail costs. To protect human rights elsewhere, to forgo exploitative arrangements, to support international institutions that fairly represent others' interests, all involve expenses either in the form of actual outlays or in the form of forgone potential profits. To have an obligation to form or participate in transnational movements is to have an obligation that may rival one's civic participatory duty. But all of these proposals, to varying degrees, involve weakening any necessary link between the republican ideal and patriotism as such. The patriot may be a republican, but support for the proposals sketched above derives from her republicanism, not from her patriotism. Is there any way to restore the link?

Challenging the claim that attachment to one's country weakens the motivation to be globally just, Stuart White draws attention to the 'honorific' aspect of republican patriotism. As patriots, we feel pride and shame in what our country does or has done, and so we will want occasions to feel proud about advancing our values, and to remedy our shame in betraying them (White 2003). That claim – assuming again that the patriot's motivation is of a republican kind – establishes an important link between patriotism and a desire to promote global justice. The link between past and present is perhaps particularly strong in 'shame' cases in which one's *patria* has committed wrongs in the past by dominating weaker countries, so that one's identification with one's own *patria* is strongly tied to a desire to make amends. Here, though, one might wonder how essential the positive or 'honorific' aspect is. Pride and shame are both honorific matters, but they are not morally symmetrical. The equivalence assumed here between pride and shame is potentially misleading. For nothing necessarily follows, morally speaking, from good achievements: praise by others or one's own self-satisfaction are entirely optional. Something *does* necessarily follow, though, from injustice, that is, the need for a remedy of some kind. If that were not so, the patriot's shame could be adequately expressed by indulging in suitably painful feelings of guilt, just as her pride would be adequately expressed in self-congratulation.

For that reason, the honorific aspect cannot be basic here. It acquires its action-guiding force from the sense that injustice has been done, which is action-guiding in a way in which the sense that justice has been done is not. There must be a criterion of injustice that is independent of patriotic values themselves, and so one need not be a patriot to endorse it. But the sense of shame, as defenders of patriotism rightly point out, is not context-independent. You can be ashamed only of what you have done, or of what has been done by those with whom you identify. In that respect, then, patriotic shame can serve to bring home to a group the injustices committed in its name.

4
Justice for Our Compatriots

'My relation of co-membership in the system of international trade with the Brazilian who grows my coffee or the Philippine worker who assembles my computer is weaker than my relation of co-membership in U.S. society with the Californian who picks my lettuce or the New Yorker who irons my shirts.'
Thomas Nagel (2005: 141)

Above we have encountered several distinct lines of thinking that sustain the idea of patriotism. There is an associative view that highlights the role of partiality in our moral lives; a nationalist view that draws attention to the importance of shared culture to our identity; and a republican view that draws upon the value of maintaining free political institutions and an ethos of shared citizenship. In this chapter, we turn to another line of thinking on which the defence of patriotism may draw. Those who have developed it may not describe themselves as 'patriots', but their arguments provide an essential resource for securing the claims of the *patria* from the critical force of cosmopolitanism. These arguments set out to rebut the claims of global justice by advancing considerations about local demands of justice that are seen as inherent in political association itself. These demands, it is urged, are neglected by cosmopolitans when they question our obligations to our country.

In this chapter we consider the two most influential justice-based arguments for acknowledging the *patria*'s claims upon us. They set out from different premises. First, there are arguments that build upon the fact that our domestic political institutions are coercive, in a way or to a degree that international institutions are not: that fact, it is claimed, obliges us to give greater consideration to those who are thus coerced. Second, there are arguments that build upon the fact that domestic political institutions, and cooperative relations among compatriots, confer benefits upon us, for which we owe a return. Both approaches, we may note, take as their starting point familiar considerations in political theory: that the fact of coercion is something that requires a very stringent kind of justification, and that the justification must demonstrate mutual benefit if it is to be compelling. So both kinds of argument have an undeniably relevant point of departure. We examine both kinds of arguments below, and conclude, however, that they are of some but only limited use to the patriot.

Coercion as a source of special concern

Political systems deliberately and in the last resort coercively impose constraints of many kinds on their citizens, and in supporting those systems citizens become complicit in what is imposed. When some citizens' interests are negatively affected by a state's policies, they can legitimately demand to be given a justification. To be damaged by some policy is not, after all, like being damaged by a natural disaster: it is to be the deliberate target of a policy choice. So, it is often argued, what one citizen can do to another, in the course of proposing and supporting policies, is constrained by what can be justified to the other (Forst 1999; Williams 2005: 4). Interestingly, this does not mean that citizens can do *less* to one another, in terms of imposing costs on them, than they can do to outsiders: in many ways they can do *more* (Goodin 1988) – they can support policies of expropriation or conscription, to mention only two examples. (We return to this point below.) But it means that they are constrained by considerations of justice that, on this view, do not apply in their dealings with outsiders. In that sense, compatriots get an important sort of preference – we owe them something that we do not owe to outsiders.

Now it must at once be noted that, in one of the most influential statements of such a view – a much-discussed article by Thomas Nagel (2005) – the term 'justice' is more narrowly used than in some other contexts. What Nagel has in mind is distributive justice, that is, the allocation of goods and opportunities according to some principle, such as equality or merit or need (in Nagel's case, equality – his case is broadly Rawlsian). It is because only states have the capacity to allocate in this manner that justice in this sense, it is claimed, can take place only within their borders. But even before we consider this view, Nagel's discussion insists on various ways in which justice more broadly conceived has a global place. Members of rich countries have a humanitarian *duty* to remedy severe deprivation in impoverished countries (Nagel 2005: 119); they have a further duty to rescue victims of oppression by admitting refugees (130); they are permitted to encourage other countries to become just (135); they should play a fair part in securing the provision of global public goods, such as environmental goods (136); they have a duty of 'decency' to avoid exploiting weaker societies (143); they are obliged not to support conditions that lead to dictatorship in other countries and also to support institutions, such as an international criminal court, that can punish and deter atrocities (143, 147). So whatever weight this view is thought to give to the claims of compatriot preference is going to be limited, from the very outset, by all these considerations. Whatever preference we think we can justifiably give to our compatriots, it is not going to include many things that countries currently do for their citizens at other countries' expense. The patriot could find no support here for compatriot-favouring practices that would involve ignoring the need for humanitarian assistance, barring (one's share of) refugees, exporting pollution, conducting unfair trading practices, or failing to pay one's share of the cost of supporting a rule-governed international order. So some of the more aggressive forms of compatriot preference are ruled out even before we get to Nagel's core thesis.

What, though, of the core thesis? Even with the above limiting conditions, it is strong enough. It means that while we must be concerned about inequality among our compatriots, and support institutions and policies that diminish it, we are not in the same way to be concerned about inequalities among nations. So, for example, we would be justified in taking steps to reduce inequality in our own country that had the predictable effect of increasing the inequality between our country and other countries, provided only that this would not violate any of the limiting conditions sketched above. We should not, for example, sell arms to dictatorships even if this provided employment in our own manufacturing sector; but we could provide support to, say, our own agricultural sector, to the benefit of our compatriots in that sector, even if this were to make other countries' agricultural exports less competitive. What might be the most important objections to that view?

The first objection relies on a broader idea of coercion than Nagel relies upon. His idea of coercion is too narrowly focused on what states do. To require someone to do something or not to do it under threat of formal sanction is indeed a form of coercion. But people are also coerced by circumstances that result from others' actions, even when no single actor can be identified and even when there is no formal threat. In that sense the global economy as a whole may be seen as a coercive system that deeply constrains freedom, and often in very uneven ways. Moreover, in the global system there *are* institutions that on the face of things at least match the state-like model of coercion: notoriously, the IMF has frequently imposed conditions on borrowers who have little option but to comply. Taking the latter point first, Nagel seeks to meet it in a way that seems to reproduce the statist framework in a question-begging way. Requirements such as IMF structural adjustment programmes are not imposed 'in the name of' the citizens who are required to abide by them, but are, rather, imposed only through the mediating agency of their state (Nagel 2005: 138). That distinction has force only if one is predisposed to think that what is done within a formal political structure has a different character from what is done otherwise. It does have a different character in several ways, we might admit, but the differences do not clearly bear on whether an act should be seen as coercive.

The former point, however – about informal coercion – seems less conclusive. One critic introduces the category of 'interactional coercion' to cover the situations involved here. She defines it as follows: 'An agent A coerces another agent B if A foreseeably and avoidably places nontrivial constraints on B's freedom, compared to B's freedom in the absence of A's intervention (other things being equal)' (Valentini 2011: 210). This achieves the needed breadth, but at a cost. It would seem, for example, to apply to A's being the success-ful bidder in a house purchase, thus nontrivially constraining B's freedom to acquire the house. Of course, that should lead us to question what freedom B could be said legitimately to have (presumably to bid, not to acquire), but in real-world cases what legitimate freedom either party could be said to have may in turn depend on our view of justice. Do third-world farmers have a freedom to export which is constrained by first-world agricultural policies? And if so, how much freedom? A similar kind of indeterminacy is introduced by the 'avoidability' condition – A coerces B only if his action is avoidable. But there is little consensus on what is and is not avoidable in the global economy, or on what cost we can require people to bear in order to avoid doing something. In short, this kind of critique could be charged with the same mistake as Nagel's argument, that is, of tailoring the idea of coercion to the preferred idea of justice.

A second objection draws attention to the fact that the state system is itself coercive in nature: for states have borders that they protect coercively. The debate here is carried out on the terrain of immigration policy; but of course, the implica-tions for global justice are very broad, since it is only by virtue of controlling membership that states can have an incentive to appropriate goods for their own population. It is Nagel's view that a state needs to justify its immigration policy only to its own citizens (Nagel 2005: 130). Why, though? The question needs asking because of a background principle of (demo-cratic) justice that tells us that all those affected by a policy are owed a justification. Mexicans are deeply affected, in a negative way, by US immigration policy, but as things stand there is no requirement that the US government provide any justification, nor any institutional mechanism (such as representation) through which a justification could be demanded. (For proposals see Koenig-Archibugi 2012.) So the excluded are essentially coerced, 'subject[ed] to the will of another' in a unilateral way that denies their status as autonomous beings (Abizadeh 2008: 39). Against this view, the need for a distinction between *coercion* and *prevention* is urged (Miller 2010). We do not coerce someone if we simply prevent them from exercising one among several options that they have; if I prevent a neighbour from entering my house (as I do whenever I lock the door) I am not being coercive, which is of course a different matter from using coercive measures if someone tried to break in. There is surely a significant difference here. But the example depends on our already agreeing that I am in rightful possession of a private good, i.e., my house, while we cannot assume that the state is in rightful and exclusive control of its territory, which is what is in question. Perhaps I should be said to be coercing my neighbour if, for example, I had kidnapped his children and was preventing him from entering to rescue them, taking this to be his only reasonable option. Once again, though, it does not seem that how we define coercion is going to settle the issue of justice. We need to know what options people need to have and what rights they need to have in order to realize them.

Because these objections may be inconclusive, the third objection to be considered here may be the most important. Perhaps we have no way of satisfactorily defining coercion that does not depend on a background idea of what is just. But all the same, there are serious grounds for questioning Nagel's claim that justice becomes a possible topic only after political order has been established, so that institutions are available for the coordinating functions that justice needs. This leads to the bleak claim that, since order precedes justice, not the other way around, the world may need to go through a phase of global tyranny before justice can find global application. But on the normative plane, the objection to this is surely provided by Kant (1970: 137). We should conceive of states as organizations that respond to a prior need for justice, so that we have a prior *duty* to create them when interactions among people become frequent and consequential enough to require ordering. Nagel's own case, it may be mentioned, itself relies upon some such argument in representing states as responses to a prior problem of mutual assurance (Nagel 2005: 115–16). It is unnecessary to suppose that, in the present global context, the response to frequent and consequential interactions among countries must be to create a world state: the more general logic applies, that is, that when interactions give rise to situations in which interests conflict there is a secondary duty to create institutions (not necessarily states) that will regulate them.

What would just regulation be like? We do not need to commit to a particular answer in order to reject the claim that the question should not be raised until institutions are in place. That is enough to undermine the view that what we do for compatriots is pre-emptively shielded from considerations about what justice might require us to do for outsiders, sometimes, one would expect, at compatriots' expense.

Benefit-based arguments

We now turn to the 'benefits' approach, distinguishing between three variants. The first builds upon what we may term 'vertical' benefits, benefits that the political society and its institutions confer upon us in a unilateral fashion. The second builds upon 'horizontal' benefits, or those benefits that compatriots confer upon one another in a mutual way. The third builds upon the benefits that we receive in the course of placing burdens upon others.

The first version was given its classical statement in Plato's *Crito* dialogue, which is presented as an account of a conversation between Socrates and friends who attempt to persuade him to escape from jail and thus avoid his death sentence. In reply to their urging, Socrates offers an uncompromising defence of his duty to his city, Athens, based (largely) upon the benefits that Athens has conferred on him, benefits that include his life itself, as well as the culture that shaped his upbringing. He imagines the city's laws speaking to him: 'Did we not give you life in the first place? Was it not through us that your father married your mother and begot you?', and 'Are you not grateful to those of us laws which were instituted ... for requiring your father to give you a cultural and physical education?' (Plato 1961: 35–6). Socrates readily agrees, rather too readily, in the view of countless later political theorists who recommend a much more limited account of what we owe to political society. Gratitude counts for something, to be sure, but for how much? To the point of requiring us to give our lives? Might we not have sufficiently repaid any debt already, by for example serving in the army (as Socrates himself had done)? Do we owe gratitude to an agent for doing what its role requires? More fundamentally still, the very idea that the simple receipt of benefits creates obligations has been challenged, notably in a famous passage in Robert Nozick's *Anarchy, State and Utopia* (1974: 93–4). Nozick imagines that you have taken up residence in a community in which a public amenity (let's say, news and music broadcasts) is provided by community volunteers. You enjoy the amenity, but does it follow that, when the volunteers come to your door to request help, you are obliged to play your part in providing the service? Surely not, Nozick suggests. You might after all prefer to have no service at all if required to contribute to it, even though you would prefer a service to which you did not have to contribute to having no service at all. Just because someone welcomes a free good, we cannot infer that they would be willing to pay for it.

However, Socrates' argument quickly takes a second tack, introducing the claim that he has not only *received* the benefits of city membership, but has in some sense actively *accepted* them. The laws speak again: 'any Athenian, on attaining to manhood and seeing for himself the political organization of the state and us its laws, is permitted, if he is not satisfied with us, to take his property and go away wherever he likes' (36–7). So, by not leaving, Socrates has bound himself in a way that active acceptance rather than passive receipt can bring about. Now there would certainly seem to be an important distinction here somewhere: consenting to something is one of the clearest ways in which one acquires an obligation. But where is the line between mere acceptance and obligation-creating consent? The history of political thought suggests the difficulty of drawing the line. Famously, John Locke, like Socrates, took the fact of not exiting to amount to a kind of binding though 'tacit' consent (Locke 1980: 64);

no less famously, David Hume took Locke to task for ignoring the deterrent or even prohibitive cost of leaving, as a factor that casts doubt on the supposed voluntariness of staying (Hume 1947: 155–6). More recently, some very ingenious political theorizing has sought to support Socrates' or Locke's side of the issue by suggesting that even unsought benefits may (sometimes) be said to be accepted, and so to give rise to obligations (Butt 2014). Suppose your neighbour hires a painter to paint his house, but the painter gets the address wrong and paints your house by mistake (in a colour that you like) – shouldn't you pay the bill? If you're in doubt, imagine that you actually sent an order to a painter to paint your house (in that colour) but that the order went astray, while your neighbour's painter, as before, got the address wrong, and painted your house? Surely then you should pay the bill? Probably 'yes', but this seems to stretch the idea of an unsought benefit to breaking point – you sought the benefit, and you got it, although the causal connection was of a really unusual kind.

So the unilateral version, in which you receive or accept benefits, may be unpersuasive, or at least inconclusive. But it is perhaps more usual to appeal to the second version of the benefits view: to the idea of *mutual* benefits. The underlying model here is a very powerful and influential one. It was given deeply effective expression by John Rawls in *A Theory of Justice* and later works. A political society is 'a cooperative venture for mutual advantage' (Rawls 1971: 4), and because the venture is marked by conflicting as well as by complementary interests, its participants recognize the need for allocative rules that fairly assign shares in the opportunities that the society affords and the goods that their cooperation gives rise to. Imagining each individual as a participant in this venture, it is an easy step to the view that he or she has special obligations to other participants, obligations that are not owed to people who are outside the boundaries of their own joint scheme of social and political relations. What we owe to people outside that scheme is thus limited by what we need in order to meet the mutual demands that apply within it.

On this model, then, we have a principled way to meet the objection that, in giving preference to our compatriots, we are guilty of favouritism and moral arbitrariness: we are not, we may reply, because we are simply responding to benefits that we have received from some (compatriots) but not from others (outsiders). But the use that we can make of that reply is limited, for at least three reasons.

First, as we can see from examining the distribution of resources within political society, the principle of mutual benefit is not the only normative model. There are non-contributors, or, if that is too summary a description, there are compatriots who necessarily consume more resources than they contribute, but to whom, nevertheless, and surely rightly, we devote public resources. These are the impaired people who may lead valuable lives but whose value does not lie in contributing to the exchange of items of measurable value that together comprise a joint product. It is an open question whether or not such impairment undermines 'the entire structure' of Rawls's view and, more generally, of 'basing principles of justice on reciprocity' (Nussbaum 2006: 145); but it does at least cast doubt on the validity of taking mutual advantage to be the exclusive foundation for what we owe. And that in turn, of course, casts doubt on the idea that considerations of mutual advantage can be exhaustive of what is owed.

Second, while we can if we wish take a current time-slice picture of a society and envisage it as (or basically as) a cooperative venture among compatriots, the reality is that a society has a history. The capital investments built into the goods that contemporaries exchange among themselves, and the institutions (laws of contract, banks, stock exchanges, regulations) permitting that process, are inherited. Those who benefit from those exchanges, then, are benefiting in a unilateral fashion from other people – past generations – who are not themselves in a position to benefit. Of course, we might say, that is just a fact of life: time goes in one direction so that we cannot benefit those who have benefited us – so what of it? What follows is that the participants in a relatively wealthy national economy cannot claim that their joint product is *their own* product in a way that obviously excludes the claims of others. They could do so if they reimagined themselves as parts of a sort of timeless organic whole, everything produced by (say) 'France' belonging to French people by virtue of their essential Frenchness, but then we would have entirely abandoned the mutual advantage model for another (and much more questionable collectivist) one – one in which our compatriots would include our ancestors.

Third, the mutual-advantage model for compatriot preference is at least complicated, and perhaps entirely undermined, by the facts of global interdependence. Mutual advantage doesn't track relations within any society, it was claimed above; and it does track relations among societies. Members of different political societies, as investors or entrepreneurs or workers, derive advantages from one another – or else they would not interact. A different question, of course, is whether or not their interactions are fair: we do not have to accept that any interaction is fair if it is mutually advantageous, for it is open to us to argue that even if exchange is mutually advantageous the terms of exchange may make it exploitative (Sample 2003); besides, the considerations here apply within national borders as well as between them, so if exploitative transnational exchanges do not count as mutually advantageous ones then domestic ones do not either, and so relations among compatriots cease to be distinctive for another reason.

The final theme to be discussed here concerns the relation among benefits and burdens. To recapitulate: you can be said to be obliged because you have received a benefit, or because you are part of a systemic exchange of benefits; the third and last idea is that you are placed under an obligation by receiving a benefit that burdens others. Its relevance to the theme of compatriot preference is clear. Suppose that, as a participant in your political society, you receive benefits that come at the expense of other members of your society: would it not follow that, for that reason, you have special obligations to those other members that you do not owe to outsiders? On the surface, that claim looks plausible. But, first, it weakens when explored, and, second, to the extent that it has force it does not track national membership.

Suppose you are a recent immigrant and you open a corner shop; you live frugally, work long hours, your family members contribute unpaid labour, you succeed, and in doing so drive a nearby store out of business. Or, suppose you are a good student, you study hard to get a strong academic record and to do well in the law school exam, and you win a place, thus excluding another applicant from admission. You go on to become wealthy while the excluded applicant does not. Both of these count as 'harms', by the way, according to J. S. Mill himself (1998: 105). In both cases you have received a benefit that necessarily carries with it a burden to be suffered by someone else. Does that benefit create an obligation on your part? Surely that depends on the background rules. In a market society, and in a society with competitive examinations, winners owe nothing to losers. It is the system of rules that we should evaluate as being fair or unfair, not the benefits that some gain. So it is not the winning of a benefit that gives rise to an obligation to make redress to the loser. If it gives rise to any obligation, it would be an obligation to consider whether the system of competition is fair and whether losers are suitably shielded from the worst effects of loss. And as people concerned about justice we all would have that obligation, not just the beneficiaries.

Now we could say, of course, that the beneficiaries are in an especially good position to respond to loss, having – by definition! – benefits of a material kind in their hands. Once again, though, that depends on whether or not their possession of those benefits is fair in terms of background rules of justice. Surely the immigrant corner-shop owner does not have to compensate a failed competitor. Moreover, that idea shifts the ground of obligation radically, toward the quite different view that whoever has the capacity owes some kind of aid to those who suffer deprivation. That principle, it is clear, would take us very far away from the idea of compatriot preference. It tells us, to the contrary, that wealthy societies, by virtue of possessing capacity, owe assistance to poor societies, not at all that members of wealthy societies have special obligations to one another. And indeed, the former view is persuasively advanced, in, for example, the context of environmental ethics: societies that can forgo luxuries carry a higher moral burden, in terms of reducing emissions, than societies that would have to forgo subsistence (Shue 1993).

The final brief consideration here is that what we may call a benefit + burden thesis – the view that those who enjoy benefits have strong obligations to those who bear resulting burdens – would quite obviously be transnational, rather than national, in its application. As we saw in considering the 'coercion' thesis above, whether we take a narrow or a broader view of what coercion means does not touch the fact that the pursuit of benefits by some countries imposes burdens on other countries, often in systematic ways. So such a thesis, far from licensing special concern for compatriots, would actually strengthen the cosmopolitan objection to whatever merit remains in the narrow-coercion view.

Finally, above we mentioned Robert Goodin's important point that in many ways our treatment of compatriots is more demanding than our treatment of outsiders. State institutions permit us – in both the normative and the practical senses of that term – to impose webs of regulation upon them that limit their freedom. That point bears upon both of the main themes in this chapter. We can do so because states have the power to coerce, in the narrow sense; and in doing so we deliberately allocate benefits and burdens among ourselves. This systematic and often minute application of mutual power will obviously give rise to special concern. Because it is deliberate, it forces choices. We have to choose tax regimes that incentivize some lives and disincentivize others, we have to balance the claims of producers and consumers and of different subnational regions, we have to weigh the competing demands of service provision in health and education, we have to reflect on issues of intergenerational fairness, and so on. Patriots, or even just good citizens, will naturally be deeply concerned with the overall success of this morally demanding process. But it is not the seriousness of the impact of this process that distinguishes it from the impact of our decisions on outsiders, which are equally serious even if (frequently) non-deliberate. What makes the process distinctive is that we already have in place institutional structures and a political culture that press us to justify what we are doing. That does not mean that what happens to outsiders needs no justification, and nothing discussed in this chapter successfully deflects the cosmopolitan demand that institutions and culture should change in ways that tend to diminish the currently substantial distance between what we owe to insiders and what we owe to those outside our *patria*.

Conclusion: A
Subsidiarity Defence

We introduced this book with three historical cases exemplifying different understandings of patriotism. First, Richard Price's Stoic universalism emphasizes our world citizenship while acknowledging love of country as both a widely held sentiment and a means of promoting the good of humanity. But Price also recommends republican citizen participation in defending free institutions: here his republican patriotism amounts to a defence of liberty and a call to his compatriots to improve their country by realizing its proud revolutionary heritage. Second, the New York *Manual of Patriotism* puts reverential story-telling, political obedience and respect for the flag at the core of love of country. And third, Alasdair MacIntyre explicitly rejects moral universalism such as one finds in Price, defending instead love of country as part of an allegedly well-grounded commitment to our moral community. The *Manual's* approach is decidedly less critical than Price's, whereas MacIntyre allows patriotic self-criticism while limiting it to competing appeals to the best self-understanding of one's country.

We began, then, with cosmopolitans, republicans and celebratory and communitarian patriots. To clarify our thinking about inevitably controversial moral and political ideas, we can appeal to a distinction between a concept or core idea and a conception or interpretation of that concept (Rawls 1971: 5–6). The concept of patriotism used by all contributors to the discussion includes love and loyalty to country, special concern for compatriots, and acceptance of duties as part of that love, loyalty and concern. But that core concept or idea of patriotism can be interpreted in many ways. Different conceptions interpret key terms differently and defend their interpretations with a range of distinctive arguments. For instance, competing conceptions give different answers to questions about the meaning of '*patria*' or 'country', emphasizing the political or the cultural or some combination of the two. Or, again, the point and purpose of patriotism could be to promote some universal ideal like freedom or well-being, or it could be understood as part of a nation-building or community-promoting project.

There are conceptions of patriotism based on essentially political values, whether these take a republican form, as in Price and the neo-Roman tradition, or a constitutionalist form of the kind recommended by Habermas and often accepted by civic or liberal nationalists; there are nationalist forms, some drawing on long-shared histories, real or imagined, and also nation-*building* forms, either assigning the *patria* to a family of other important partial associations, or more strongly (as in MacIntyre) assigning it to a uniquely potent communitarian influence.

We need to tread carefully, of course, in reaching conclusions about such a family of conceptions. But there is one general issue, already touched on in the Introduction, that in one way or another all patriotisms raise: they conjoin a fact and a value – the fact of belonging, and whichever value is picked out by the conception in question. We can then ask: to which are we fundamentally attached? Whichever answer we give seems to lead to a major objection. Our present purpose is to lay out a view of patriotism that gives it a significant moral place despite these objections.

Objection 1 is that if we assign independent moral weight to patriotism we run the risk of turning it into a form of what Eamonn Callan (2006) calls 'idolatry', in the rather precise sense that it substitutes a material thing for a value that properly lies beyond it as an object of attachment or love. We would be (mistakenly) loving our country rather than loving the values or ideals that might make it worthy of our love. Objection 2 is that if indeed, on the other hand, we love our country if and just because it advances values or ideals of a general kind, then essentially we have emptied the idea of patriotism of any moral significance of its own. Do the grounds of these objections simply exhaust the moral possibilities, so that patriotism must fail to qualify as a moral good for one or other reason?

We believe that this conclusion can and should be avoided, and in support of our view we shall work our way toward the idea of *subsidiarity*. That idea has a long history (Føllesdal 1998), not all of which is relevant here, but its general point is to draw attention to the question of properly assigning responsibility in a spatial or organizational context. Theorists of subsidiarity maintain that a task should be transferred upwards from a local to a larger level of administration if and only if it can better be accomplished there: it contains, then, a certain bias toward the local, in that it is the denial of local jurisdiction that needs to be justified. That justification is standardly sought in terms of efficiency issues: can a service be more effectively provided at one level than another? But here we propose a moralized version of subsidiarity. Given that we face choices about where to locate our moral identification, our view about what commitments matter to us, is there any reason to favour the local, and, of course, in particular, the *patria*? It should go without saying, given some of the discussion in the chapters above, that psychological reasons are not what we are looking for here, any more than efficiency reasons. We are looking for a moral reason to value one's *patria* – one that neither idolizes it nor empties it of any intrinsic importance.

Making sense of 'association'

In Chapter 1 we introduced the topic of 'associative morality', that is, the view that duties have their source in the relationships among members of associations such as families, enterprises of all kinds, and countries. That view is a natural resource if we want to make moral sense of patriotism, especially; for other kinds of association may often have their origin in some pre-associative value or aim that gives them a justification – so a book club, for example, serves a purpose that its members entertained before it existed. But it is an arbitrary matter that one should be born in one country rather than another, and if belonging to it can be said to have some value then that must be because of what happens subsequently. Although it is an arbitrary matter that one should belong to one country rather than another, the fact of belonging may, as nationalists point out, give rise to important obligations that are not arbitrary at all. So it seems natural to say that, if patriotism is a value, then it must be an associative one, because it cannot be anything else.

But in discussing the associative view, we drew attention to some exaggerated claims that are made for it, in particular in the course of trying to shield associative duties from the sort of scrutiny that other views of morality might prompt. So we pointed out, for example, what we may term the 'moral learning fallacy' or the claim that because moral beliefs arise in the context of local associations their content cannot be generalized beyond those associations – as though being, say, British, and learning about right and wrong in the context of a particular national culture, one would be incapable of taking what one has learned and applying it more generally. We drew attention, too, to the difference between motivation and justification: just because we hold that it is a generally good thing that parents should take care of their children, that does not mean that they take care of them out of obedience to a general rule, as opposed to taking care of them because they love them. And we drew attention to the mistake involved in believing that, because local practices cannot be predicted from general purposes, they cannot be measured in terms of how well they serve a general purpose. From the idea that 'decency' is a general value, for example, we cannot predict how decency in dress will be defined in Tehran and San Diego, but that does not mean that the very different standards or measures of acceptable exposure in play in these two places cannot be said to reflect a single criterion for what is to be measured.

For all such reasons, then, we should resist any strong claim that local loyalties are morally self-sufficient in a way that excludes evaluation. But all the same, we cannot deny that they have serious moral weight. Consider cases in which people display associative virtues, such as loyalty and honesty, in a bad cause. Some views, it is true, would seem to exclude the very possibility of that happening: thus David Miller, for example, writes that special duties 'arise only from relationships that are intrinsically valuable' and that a condition for accepting such duties is that 'the attachments that ground them should not inherently involve injustice' (Miller 2005: 66); but that seems questionable at least. Could one not be a loyal and honest member of a crime syndicate, for example? One thinks of Tom the mob lawyer in *The Godfather* movies. Or one could be a very correct member of a profession that comes to be co-opted for evil ends – there must have been many members of the officer class in Nazi Germany who matched this description. If we accept that a treacherous Mafioso lawyer or a vicious army officer would fall lower in our estimation than their upright counterparts, then we must be supposing that the good associative traits make some significant difference. That may even be so in a remarkable case that is the subject of a recent study (Pauer-Studer and Velleman 2015): that of Konrad Morgen, a judge in the legal branch of the SS who spent his war prosecuting financial irregularities in the death camps: he displayed great probity, though admittedly this very extreme case stretches the claim made here to the limit, or maybe beyond.

What about the converse case, in which one breaks a valuable associative rule in order to advance a larger end? Suppose you deceive a friend or good neighbour in order to conceal the fact that you are sheltering innocent victims of persecution in your basement? One can believe that this was unequivocally the right thing to do without believing that the duty not to deceive simply evaporated, as opposed to being overridden by something still more important; so it would not be absurd, though probably not obligatory, to apologize to the neighbour when the danger was long over.

The conclusion, then, is that while associative duties to compatriots and others are not insulated from other moral considerations, they have their own moral weight. But now let us turn the tables and ask how well the universalist can cope with issues such as this. The basic strategy must be to represent local duties as ways of giving effect to some purpose of more-than-local value. Important examples include Brian Barry's model (discussed above) of 'second-order impartiality' – it is often desirable from an impartial point of view that tasks should be carried out by people with strongly partial feelings (Barry 1995: 11–12). Martha Nussbaum (1996: 13) cites the example of child care, arguing, surely persuasively, that the world goes better if parents devote their (primary) attention to their own children rather than to spatially and emotionally distant ones. And Robert Goodin (1988), in a more fully worked-out treatment that deals specifically with nations, argues that local national jurisdictions should be regarded as ways of 'assigning' general human duties to agents with defined responsibilities. This is the 'lifeguard' model: we all have duties to rescue drowning people, but it is a good thing if the duties are assigned to specialists on our behalf. To the objection that a great many local political institutions – unlike lifeguards, or so one would hope – are actually unable to perform their 'assigned' functions, Goodin replies that in that case successful states with more resources are obliged to give them the means to do so.

Now this may provide a very useful way of thinking about global justice in a world made up of states: it both makes sense of states as agents of general human well-being, and supports a normative programme that addresses the huge inequalities in present state capacity. But from the standpoint of the issue under discussion here, all such approaches endorse local associative attachments only on condition that they satisfy some universal criterion. Parent–child ties are valuable only if and to the extent that the parents come up to some mark; political societies are valuable only if and to the extent that they meet some benchmark of efficiency in promoting human well-being. So do such views recognize associative ties in the way that one might want them to?

Here are two objections. One is an objection that we have encountered already: that of course we could love our country if all it did was what was required of it from a universal point of view. But then, what we would be loving would be the requirements of that point of view, not the *patria* as such. If you love something only on condition that it has some quality, then what you love is that quality (Nozick 1974: 168). If you love your partner *because* she has such blue eyes, then you should change her for someone who has still bluer ones. A second, related, objection is that on a robustly universalist view it would seem to be a matter of indifference that some well-being-promoting function happens to be carried out at one level rather than another. That is, of course, unfaithful to the ways in which people think about both their families and their countries. They want their well-being to be promoted within their associations, and if theory is indifferent on the question of where services come from then it is simply out of touch with the psychology of belonging. No doubt in extreme cases people would be glad to have services from any source whatsoever, local or otherwise, but extreme cases are a poor guide to the normal contexts of life.

Subsidiarity

Samuel Scheffler calls the topic described immediately above a 'reductive dilemma' (2010: 287–8). If you love your country because it embodies some valuable attribute, then your love of it 'reduces' to that, just as, if you say you support party P1 because it advances goal G, then you need a very good reason not to switch to party P2 if it compellingly offers better reasons to be an electoral path to G. Likewise, if you identify with and promote the cause of your country because it embodies values V1 and V2, then your attachment to its cause depends on its actually embodying V1 and V2 better than some other country does. And as we have seen, Alasdair MacIntyre rightly denies that that would be patriotism. Is there a way out of the 'reductive dilemma'?

A very useful way forward is offered by Scheffler's treatment of two contexts that, he argues, point in different normative directions: those of 'culture' and 'tradition'. In the former context, he regards the dilemma as fatal to culturalist claims: either you believe the claims are sustainable on their merits outside the culture, or else you are taking an arbitrarily self-referential stance, one that amounts, ultimately, to saying: I believe it because it is my belief. But in the context of 'tradition', Scheffler offers a thought-provoking defence, claiming that there are several reasons to believe that it is an idea with its own normative force, independent of the values that we endorse in it. Some of these reasons, we shall suggest, apply to patriotism(s) too: a patriotism may be normatively neutral, like culture, or normatively strong, as (some) traditions are.

'Values, ideals and principles', Scheffler points out, 'are not self-interpreting', and we benefit from 'a well-developed body of advice and instruction about how to interpret those values and how best to apply them to the concrete circumstances of daily life'. Moreover, 'many values, principles and norms are "imperfect" in the Kantian sense; that is, they articulate norms of living with which we are supposed to comply, but these norms leave the timing and manner of our compliance up to us' (Scheffler 2010: 292). Traditions confer these benefits, Scheffler claims, but there are two important ways in which what he claims may illuminate patriotism too. Richard Bellamy's book, *Liberalism and Modern Society* (1992), explored the ways in which the different origins and development of the liberal tradition in Britain, France, Italy and Germany have given adherents of that tradition different points of reference and different sensitivities that both colour its application and tie it to concrete experience in ways that a formal statement of 'the meaning of liberalism' would not do. Similarly, democrats in those and other countries identify the meaning of 'democracy' with particular distinctive institutions, practices and memories that shape its political interpretation. It is true that, as we noted above in Chapter 1, those institutions and practices would not be valued if they were not taken to embody a background value. But here the other side of that point needs to be made, that is, that one would not know how to be a democrat without some template or other enabling one to coordinate action with others and to define legitimate outcomes. Consider, for example, the very different views of the role of courts in a democratic system, American constitutionalism endorsing judicial review of legislation, 'Westminster' systems endorsing scepticism about it: attachment to one political tradition or another provides a starting point for finding accommodation with others within that tradition, even though the theory of democracy itself may be inconclusive on the matter (Waldron 1993: 392–421; Holmes 1995: chapter 5).

As for the second part of Scheffler's claim here, over and above what principles dictate, much that is good is discretionary. Let us suppose, surely not unreasonably, that over and above what is demanded by human rights there are benefits that we should confer on others: for example, we should as far as possible avoid disappointing established expectations, or compensate for their defeat, even though the disappointed had no actual right in the matter. Or, to take a more specific example, there may be no reasons in general theories of justice why political societies should pay special attention to the fate of valuable cultural items produced within their own territory. Perhaps a sort of Rawlsian difference principle for artefacts would tell us to preserve the 'worst-off' items at most risk, wherever they happen to be from. But it is a fair bet that more items get protected because of a sense, discretionary from a strictly moral point of view, that members of political societies feel an identification with the achievements of their predecessors and attach value to the things that they made, just as it is a fair bet that people are likely to be shielded from the effects of disappointed but non-rightful expectations if others attach value to their connection with them.

Now these considerations may simply seem, at first glance, to take us back to the reductive dilemma. If it is indeed a good thing, from a practical point of view, that abstract political principles should be concretized in particular local ways, and if it is a good thing that matters of discretionary value should be taken up by local sentiment rather than being neglected, then are we not back on cosmopolitan terrain? Are we not back, in effect, to second-order impartiality, that is, saying that the world goes better from a global point of view if people act locally? Here, though, two other valuable considerations introduced by Scheffler may obstruct this reductive move. The first is that local engagement may often draw upon shared identity. That I am now doing something that chimes with what valued others have done is itself a reason for doing it (Scheffler 2010: 294). It is not a matter of being extraneously motivated – in a psychological sense – to do what is right; it is *another reason* to do it, a reason drawn from the values of loyalty and integrity. Those values may not, all things considered, license doing what was wrong, but they may overdetermine doing what is right. The second consideration is that one may have reason to *regard as valuable* something that one does not oneself *value* (293). A robust cosmopolitan may object and say, I can justify all the things that are claimed for patriotism from a strictly impartial point of view; so from the standpoint of my world-view I do not value patriotism. But that does not mean she should not regard patriotism as something that on balance may be more valuable than not. To be sure, that is not enough to make patriotism an obligatory value, for on this argument it is clearly not a unique way of realizing goods, but it is enough to make it a permissible one, referring here again to an important distinction made by Igor Primoratz (in Kleinig et al. 2015: 127–9).

This brings us back to the idea of subsidiarity with which we began this chapter. From a robust cosmopolitan point of view, as we saw, it could be a matter of indifference whether some necessary good were to be provided by one level of organization or another. What matters is simply that the good be delivered and enjoyed. Given the considerations that we have outlined above, that view may need correction or qualification. It may be, in at least some important cases, that the good in question is undeliverable, because undefinable, without local context; that the good is highly desirable, without however being required by justice; that, given rather well-established facts about human behaviour, we attach value to arrangements that we have no reasonable expectation of replacing; that it is a good thing if what should be done is reinforced by a sense that in doing it one is also exemplifying loyalty to valued others. That is a mixed bag of considerations, of course. But perhaps it is not surprising that there should be no single decisive answer to the question of where powers should be located and which location should attract people's attachment. We have only tried to show that it may not be a matter of indifference that a good is provided by one level of organization rather than another, for there may often be reasons to favour its local provision. To that extent, we may regard patriotism as valuable, and respect those who value it.

The patriotic society and its enemies

If the subsidiarity defence has merit, then we may see value in there being relatively local levels of association, including the *patria*, at which humanly valuable goods are provided and pursued. To what extent, though, does this serve to protect patriotism from its most severe critics? The limited claims made above clearly do not meet the most hostile objections to patriotism, for we have claimed only that in addition to providing humanly valuable goods, the *patria* may do so in the course of and by way of embodying distinctive locally valuable goods. But of course, what the severest critics maintain is that far from delivering humanly valuable goods, albeit often in local form, attachment to the *patria* tends systematically to *betray* humanly valuable goods in favour of particular and destructive ones. What we have is not a possible and benign relationship of subsidiarity, they claim, but one of actual and malign conflict. In this final section, we consider and respond to three important versions of this critique.

The first is Leo Tolstoy's, perhaps the most thoroughgoing, uncompromising and rhetorically brilliant attack on patriotism ever written. In two articles (1894, 1900), he sets out a devastating critique that focuses essentially on the ways in which patriotic feeling lends itself to war. 'Patriotism is in our time an unnatural, irrational, and harmful sentiment, which causes the greater part of those calamities from which humanity suffers ... this sentiment ought not to be cultivated, as it now is, but on the contrary, ought to be repressed with all means that sensible people can command.' It is 'in our time ... unnatural' because today the nations 'live among themselves in peaceful, mutually advantageous, amicable, industrial, commercial, mental relations, which they have no reason and no need to violate'. That is true, however, only of 'the nations, not the governments'. For the ruling classes (a broadly understood term) have a vested interest in provoking and fostering sentiments that support the power of the state (Tolstoy 1900: 1, 3). Let the states stop doing all that they do 'in order to rouse patriotism, loyalty, and submission in Germany, France, Italy, England, and America, and we should see in how far this imaginary patriotism is characteristic of the nations of our time'. And: 'Every power is based on patriotism and the readiness of men to submit to power' (Tolstoy 1894: 21, 25).

Patriotism, then, is to be rejected because it is the nexus between the state and war, and any good that it might do (even if Tolstoy could somehow be made to agree that it did any good at all) would be overwhelmed by the cruelty and slaughter that it unleashed. But the idea of an essential nexus between the state and war is dubious. The anthropologist Lawrence Keeley (1996), in a full-length comparative study, presents evidence that pre-state societies experienced a higher rate of death in war than modern societies have. Their wars were shorter, but much more frequent, and the loss of a small fraction of your population year after year soon amounts to a larger fraction than modern European states suffered over a comparable stretch of time. Moreover, Tolstoy is silent on causes of war other than state-induced ones. Remarkably, while invoking 'Christian enlightenment' (Tolstoy 1894: 23) as a moral transformation that made enmity among nations obsolete, he nowhere recognizes religious differences, either within Christianity or between Christianity and other religions, as a source of violence; violence that could perhaps in some cases have been limited by fellow-feeling among citizens. In short, patriotism is drained of any possible value by a one-dimensional critique of the state.

It is of course hardly a surprise that, as a Christian anarchist, Tolstoy should reject states. But he goes beyond anything required by either his Christianity or his anarchism by setting his face against particularity as such. 'Is it not obvious that, if at some time the peculiarities of each nation – its customs, beliefs, and language – formed an indispensable condition of the life of humanity, these same peculiarities serve in our time as the chief impediment to the realization of the ideal of brotherly union of the nations?' He goes on at once to associate the sense of peculiarity with a sense of superiority: the patriotic sense of difference 'is stupid, since it is clear that if every nation and state shall consider itself the best of nations and states, then all of them will find themselves in a gross and harmful error' (Tolstoy 1900: 1, 2). For, obviously, we cannot all be the best. But nothing in the view defended here involves competitive claims of that sort. It involves only the sense that participating in a distinctive practice can be valued as a good from the inside, and seen as valuable, sometimes, from the outside too, if the good can be affirmed from there. It would not at all have to be the case that the good affirmed had to be the best from anyone's point of view.

George Kateb's essay, 'Is Patriotism a Mistake?' (2000) – written largely as a response to the work by Viroli discussed above in Chapter 3 – is so wide-ranging that no brief response can do it justice. We shall pick out only two of its important themes: the fictitiousness objection and the 'necessary othering' hypothesis. The fictitiousness objection is easily stated. The *patria* does not exist unless it is thought to exist. 'One's country – any country – is best understood as an abstraction, for it is a compound of a few actual and many imaginary ingredients', and '[a] country is not a discernible collection of discernible individuals like a team or a faculty or a local chapter of a voluntary association' (Kateb 2000: 907). Regardless, then, of any benefits that might be thought to flow from it (and Kateb, like Tolstoy, seems to think that what mostly flows from it is not a benefit, but violence), patriotism would involve something like a disgraceful intellectual error (of which academics, in particular, should be ashamed, Kateb says). To be a patriot is to believe in something that exists only because you and others believe in it. Error or not, the claim is consistent with a well-established view about how nations came to be (Anderson 1991). But is it an error? Kateb believes that other institutions, such as teams or academic faculties, do not involve the error that infects patriotism. But surely any social institution is an artefact of joint imagination. Consider all the beliefs that we have to accept in order to see a collection of baseball players, born in various parts of the world and tradeable from team to team on the basis of complex rules, as a 'team'. Or consider all the beliefs that we have to accept, including beliefs about where definitional authority comes from, to agree that hundreds of scholars doing heterogeneous and mutually unintelligible kinds of work in a large public university constitute a single 'faculty'. Many years ago, a book by the philosopher Peter Winch (1958) drew our attention to the ways in which the reality of institutions is constituted by the beliefs of their participants. More recently, as we have noted, Yuval Noah Harari (2014) presented a case for seeing the story-telling capacity of *Homo sapiens* as essential to the species' capacity to create associations. If that is something that we need to understand about the *patria* then it does not distinguish it from any other institution. That it may do some good is not bought at the cost of self-deception any more than we could say would necessarily be so in other cases.

Kateb's other important objection is grounded in the need for patriotism to identify an Other, a different or hostile Other, with violent consequences. Here we need to mention two lines of enquiry that would have to be pursued in order to assess the force of Kateb's objection to patriotism. One is that we would need a scorecard: one that would count up the damage caused by countries' othering of each other and weigh it against the damage arising from internal othering, prevented by overcoming (for example) regional or tribal or interclass conflicts. According to statistics quoted by Robert Muchembled, homicide rates in thirteenth-century Oxford and London averaged about twenty times the twentieth-century rate in the UK, a reduction that must surely be due to the strengthening of political and legal ties (Muchembled 2012: 38). But is such a quantitative scorecard really possible? Rousseau certainly thought so, and he believed it supported the view that Kateb endorses – that states are, above all, killers of outsiders. States put an end to civil wars, Rousseau wrote (1761: 4), only to give rise to foreign wars infinitely more terrible. But that is questionable. The crude body count, at least, suggests otherwise (Rummel 1994), and, regrettable though all othering is, it may not be that patriotism is the main culprit here. Once again, as briefly noted in discussing Tolstoy above, we would need not only to balance the ways in which shared belonging impeded other internal differences against the ways in which collective belonging inspired externally directed violence, but also to weigh the contribution of other factors (religious and ideological) in explaining internal and external violence alike.

Perhaps the most influential recent academic critique of patriotism is an essay by Martha Nussbaum that became the lead chapter in a volume with critical commentaries on her view by other distinguished scholars. In her essay 'Patriotism and Cosmopolitanism' (1996), Nussbaum, drawing on a novel by the Indian author Rabindranath Tagore, depicts patriotism as a colourful but basically deceptive passion that can distract people from purposes of true value. It is essentially a school of narrowness: putting one's country first is essentially no different from, or better than, putting one's sect or one's caste first. Her sympathies seem to lie much more with ancient cosmopolitans such as the Cynics whose view of their relationship to their *patria* was, to say the least, very detached. Critics of her essay detected in it a lack of feeling for the moral content of 'love of country'. But a much more nuanced view is offered by Nussbaum in a chapter on patriotism in her later book, *Political Emotions*. For here, in line with the overall theme of that book, she gives full weight to the ways in which patriotism can embody and motivate attachment to things of general value (Nussbaum 2013: 212). Much of her chapter is devoted to 'good patriots' such as Lincoln, Martin Luther King and Gandhi, who linked love of country to great ideals such as the pursuit of equality. The constitutional patriotism of Habermas is rejected as uninspiringly bloodless, as is the somewhat similar picture of political community offered by Rawls; and now, interestingly, ancient cosmopolitanism is exemplified, not by the attractively colourful and eccentric Cynics, but by the Stoic emperor Marcus Aurelius, who is condemned as 'lonely and hollow', and as lacking in eros (223).

But while the good in patriotism is now fully acknowledged in her work, Nussbaum by no means loses sight of its potential to go bad. 'The very particularity and eroticism of patriotic love make it ripe for capture, it would seem, by darker forces in our personalities' (209). It is not, she suggests a little later, its eroticism as such that gives it this dark potential – for it is 'difficult to see what argument could be given for the claim that love is always likely to be unwise, or connected to bad policy choices' (212). Nor, it seems, is it its particularity as such that is to blame, for if it were we would also be bound to reject the even more particularistic love of family (212). What may make its particularism more perilous than family feeling, however, is that it is boundary-setting in a more basic way: it does not only place value on who is in, it can define who is in and who is out. Whereas Tolstoy places all the emphasis on the violent exclusion of foreigners from moral concern, Nussbaum stresses, rather, *internal* exclusions. We need to ensure, she writes, that 'the narrative of the nation's history and current identity is not exclusionary, not emphasizing the contribution of a single ethnic, racial, or religious group to the denigration or even omission of others' (213–14). But 'history shows many cases in which the appeal to the nation is uneven and even exclusionary, defining certain groups and people as not really part of the nation' (214), and one such case, involving the Jehovah's Witnesses and the Pledge of Allegiance in the US, is explored at length (218). Since Nussbaum's *Political Emotions* was published, a disturbing book by Robert Parkinson (2016) has argued that, from the Revolution on, the American *patria* was defined by the systematic and calculated exclusion of Blacks and native people from the political narrative.

Although the language of subsidiarity is nowhere used, the upshot of Nussbaum's account is very congenial to the view presented above. Patriotisms are acceptable if what they endorse can also be endorsed from a larger point of view. That does not mean that they are merely instrumental from the patriot's standpoint, for the patriot may well see inherent expressive value in her participation, and perhaps they can be valuably instrumental only if they are invested with ethical value (Miller 1995: 66–8). Nor does it mean that the content of patriotism must be deducible from abstract statements of value, for its content is certain to contain historically and contextually specific features. Can we ever say that endorsing it is not merely acceptable but actually required (to apply Primoratz's distinction again)? That simply cannot be so if the value of what is affirmed in it must be independently assessable, so that at least in principle it could be affirmed without patriotism. But if, as Nussbaum came to argue, there are circumstances in which values can only be realized through the medium of congenial patriotisms, then one could say that there are times when supporting a patriotic cause could be required from the standpoint of a politically aware morality, one that took account of the preconditions for joint and thus effective action.

As we have seen throughout this book, different conceptions of patriotism offer a range of supporting arguments while facing sustained criticism from alternative understandings of patriotism and from independently defended perspectives, usually representing some form of moral universalism. We hope the multifaceted character of patriotism has emerged clearly from our discussions of community, loyalty, partiality, nationalism, cosmopolitanism and republicanism, along with appeals to coercion and benefits as grounds for patriotic special concern. We have described powerful arguments pointing out the dangers of patriotic identification, and equally compelling arguments showing how associative duties to compatriots can be valuable, both in themselves and when they are impartially defensible.

References

Abizadeh, Arash (2002) 'Does Liberal Democracy Presuppose a Cultural Nation? Four Arguments', *American Political Science Review* 96 (3), 495–509.

Abizadeh, Arash (2008) 'Democratic Theory and Border Coercion: No Right to Unilaterally Control Your Own Borders', *Political Theory* 36 (1), 37–65.

Anderson, Benedict (1991) *Imagined Communities: Reflections on the Origin and Spread of Nationalism*, revised edition, London: Verso.

Appiah, Kwame Anthony (2005) *The Ethics of Identity*, Princeton: Princeton University Press.

Appiah, Kwame Anthony (2006) *Cosmopolitanism*, New York: Norton.

Appiah, Kwame Anthony (2010) *The Honor Code: How Moral Revolutions Happen*, New York: Norton.

Appiah, Kwame Anthony (2016) *Mistaken Identities*, The Reith Lectures, http://www.bbc.co.uk/programmes/b080twcz.

Baldwin, James (1955) *Notes of a Native Son*, Boston: Beacon.

Baron, Marcia (1989) 'Patriotism and "Liberal" Morality', in David Weissbord, ed., *Mind, Value, and Culture: Essays in Honor of E. M. Adams*, Atascadero: Ridgeview.

Barry, Brian (1991) *Essays in Political Theory*, Volume 1: *Democracy and Power*, Oxford: Clarendon Press.

Barry, Brian (1995) *Justice as Impartiality*, Oxford: Oxford University Press.

Bearak, Max (2016) 'Theresa May Criticized the Term "Citizen of the World," But Half the World Identifies That Way', *Washington Post*, 5 October.

Beitz, Charles (1979) *Political Theory and International Relations*, Princeton: Princeton University Press.

Bellamy, Richard (1992) *Liberalism and Modern Society*, Cambridge: Polity Press.

Blackmon, Douglas A. (2009) *Slavery by Another Name: The Re-Enslavement of Black Americans from the Civil War to World War II*, New York: Anchor.

Blake, Michael (2001) 'Distributive Justice, State Autonomy, and Coercion', *Philosophy and Public Affairs* 30, 257–96.

Bohman, James (2004) 'Republican Cosmopolitanism', *Journal of Political Philosophy* 12, 336–52.

Bromwich, David (2014) *Moral Imagination*, Princeton: Princeton University Press.

Burke, Edmund (1982) *Reflections on the Revolution in France*, London: Penguin.

Butt, Daniel (2014) ' "A Doctrine Quite New and Altogether Untenable": Defending the Beneficiary Pays Principle', *Journal of Applied Philosophy* 31 (4), 336–48.

Callan, Eamonn (2006) 'Love, Idolatry, and Patriotism', *Social Theory and Practice* 32 (4), 525–46.

Callan, Eamonn (2010) 'The Better Angels of Our Nature: Patriotism and Dirty Hands', *Journal of Political Philosophy* 18 (3), 249–70.

Caney, Simon (2008) 'Global Distributive Justice and the State', *Political Studies* 56 (3), 487–518.

Canovan, Margaret (1996) *Nationhood and Political Theory*, Cheltenham: Edward Elgar.

Colley, Linda (1992) *Britons: Forging the Nation, 1707–1837*, New Haven: Yale University Press.

Coxe, William (1790) *A Letter to the Rev. Richard Price*, London, printed for T. Cadell.

Cruft, Rowan, S. Matthew Liao and Massimo Renzo, eds (2015) *Philosophical Foundations of Human Rights*, Oxford: Oxford University Press.

De Bruin, Boudewijn (2009) 'Liberal and Republican Freedom', *Journal of Political Philosophy* 17, 418–39.

Duthille, Rémy (2012) 'Richard Price on Patriotism and Universal Benevolence', *Enlightenment and Dissent* 28 (1), 24–41.

Feinberg, Joel (1988) 'Liberalism, Community, and Tradition', *Tikkun* 3 (3), 38–41 and 116–20.

Fletcher, George (1993) *Loyalty: An Essay on the Morality of Relationships*, Oxford: Oxford University Press.

Føllesdal, Andreas (1998) 'Survey Article: Subsidiarity', *Journal of Political Philosophy* 6 (2), 190–218.

Forst, Rainer (1999) 'The Basic Right to Justification', *Constellations* 6, 35–60.

Forster, E. M. (1939) *What I Believe*, London: Hogarth Press.

Gates, Henry Louis (1998) 'The End of Loyalty', *New Yorker*, 9 March, 34–44.

Glover, Jonathan (1999) *Humanity: A Moral History of the 20th Century*, New Haven: Yale University Press.

Godwin, William (1971) *Enquiry Concerning Political Justice*, ed. K. Codell Carter, Oxford: Clarendon Press (first published 1793).

Goodin, Robert (1988) 'What Is So Special About Our Fellow-Countrymen?', *Ethics* 98, 663–86.

Habermas, Jürgen (1994) 'Citizenship and National Identity', in Bart van Steenbergen, ed., *The Condition of Citizenship*, London: Sage.

Harari, Yuval Noah (2014) *Sapiens: A Brief History of Humankind*, Toronto: McLelland and Stewart.

Hobbes, Thomas (1994) *Leviathan*, Indianapolis: Hackett (first published 1651).

Hobsbawm, Eric (1990) *Nations and Nationalism Since 1780*, Cambridge: Cambridge University Press.

Holmes, Stephen (1995) *Passions and Constraint: On the Theory of Liberal Democracy*, Chicago: University of Chicago Press.

Honohan, Iseult (2002) *Civic Republicanism*, London: Routledge.

Hume, David (1947) 'Of the Original Contract', in Ernest Barker, ed., *Social Contract: Locke, Hume, Rousseau*, London: Oxford University Press (first published 1748).

Isaac, Jeffrey C. (1988) 'Republicanism versus Liberalism? A Reconsideration', *History of Political Thought* 9, 349–77.

Ivison, Duncan (2010) 'Republican Human Rights?', *European Journal of Political Theory*, 9 (1), 31–47.

Jones, Charles (1999) *Global Justice*, Oxford: Oxford University Press.

Kahneman, Daniel (2011) *Thinking Fast and Slow*, Toronto: Doubleday Canada.

Kant, Immanuel (1970) *Political Writings*, Cambridge: Cambridge University Press.

Kateb, George (2000) 'Is Patriotism a Mistake?', *Social Research* 67 (4), 901–24.

Keeley, Lawrence (1996) *War Before Civilization*, New York: Oxford University Press.

Keller, Simon (2005) 'Patriotism as Bad Faith', *Ethics* 115 (3), 563–92.

Keller, Simon (2007) *The Limits of Loyalty*, Cambridge: Cambridge University Press.

Kennedy, John F. (1961) 'Inaugural Address of President John F. Kennedy', 20 January, jfklibrary.org.

Kleingeld, Pauline (2000) 'Kantian Patriotism', *Philosophy and Public Affairs* 29 (4), 313–41.

Kleingeld, Pauline and Eric Brown (2013) 'Cosmopolitanism', in *Stanford Encyclopedia of Philosophy*, ed. Edward N. Zalta, http:// plato.stanford.edu/archives/fall2014/entries/cosmopolitanism.

Kleinig, John, Simon Keller and Igor Primoratz (2015) *The Ethics of Patriotism: A Debate*, Chichester: Wiley Blackwell.

Knowles, Elizabeth, ed. (2004) *The Oxford Dictionary of Quotations*, sixth edition, Oxford: Oxford University Press.

Koenig-Archibugi, Mathias (2012) 'Fuzzy Citizenship in Global Society', *Journal of Political Philosophy* 20 (4), 451–80.

Kymlicka, Will (1995) *Multicultural Citizenship*, Oxford: Oxford University Press.

Kymlicka, Will (2002) *Contemporary Political Philosophy: An Introduction*, second edition, Oxford: Oxford University Press.

Kymlicka, Will (2003) 'Being Canadian', *Government and Opposition* 38 (3), 357–85.

Laborde, Cécile (2010) 'Republicanism and Global Justice: A Sketch', *European Journal of Political Theory* 9 (1), 48–69.

Lenard, Patti Tamara and Margaret Moore (2012) 'A Defence of Moderate Cosmopolitanism and/or Liberal Nationalism', in Will Kymlicka and Kathryn Walker, eds, *Rooted Cosmopolitanism: Canada and the World*, Vancouver: UBC Press.

Locke, John (1975) *An Essay Concerning Human Understanding*, Oxford: Clarendon Press (first published 1689).

Locke, John (1980) *Second Treatise of Government*, Indianapolis: Hackett (first published 1689).

Lovett, Frank (2016) 'Should Republicans be Cosmopolitans?', *Global Justice: Theory Practice Rhetoric* 9 (1), 28–46.

Macedo, Stephen (2011) 'Just Patriotism?', *Philosophy and Social Criticism* 37 (4), 413–23.

MacIntyre, Alasdair (1981) *After Virtue: A Study in Moral Theory*, London: Duckworth.

MacIntyre, Alasdair (1984) 'Is Patriotism a Virtue?', Lindley Lecture, Lawrence: University of Kansas.

Mason, Andrew (1997) 'Special Obligations to Compatriots', *Ethics* 107, 427–47.

Mele, Alfred R. (2004) 'Motivated Irrationality', in Alfred R. Mele and Piers Rawling, eds, *The Oxford Handbook of Rationality*, Oxford: Oxford University Press.

Mill, John Stuart (1884) *Three Essays on Religion*, New York: Henry Holt.

Mill, John Stuart (1998) *On Liberty and Other Essays*, ed. John Gray, Oxford: Oxford University Press.

Miller, David (1995) *On Nationality*, Oxford: Oxford University Press.

Miller, David (2005) 'Reasonable Partiality Towards Compatriots', *Ethical Theory and Moral Practice* 8 (1), 63–81.

Miller, David (2010) 'Why Immigration Controls are Not Coercive: A Reply to Arash Abizadeh', *Political Theory* 38 (1), 111–20.

Monroe, Kristen Renwick (1998) *The Heart of Altruism: Perceptions of a Common Humanity*, Princeton: Princeton University Press.

Moore, Margaret (2010) 'Defending Community: Nationalism, Patriotism and Culture', in Duncan Bell, ed., *Ethics and World Politics*, Oxford: Oxford University Press.

Muchembled, Robert (2012) *A History of Violence: From the End of the Middle Ages to the Present*, Cambridge: Polity.

Müller, Jan-Werner (2007) *Constitutional Patriotism*, Princeton: Princeton University Press.

Muthu, Sankar (2003) *Enlightenment Against Empire*, Princeton: Princeton University Press.

Nagel, Thomas (2005) 'The Problem of Global Justice', *Philosophy and Public Affairs* 33, 114–47.

Nathanson, Stephen (1993) *Patriotism, Morality, and Peace*, Lanham MD: Rowman and Littlefield.

Nathanson, Stephen (1997) 'Nationalism and the Limits of Global Humanism', in Robert McKim and Jeff McMahan, eds, *The Morality of Nationalism*, Oxford: Oxford University Press.

New York State (1900) *Manual of Patriotism*, Albany NY: Brandow Printing Company.

Nozick, Robert (1974) *Anarchy, State, and Utopia*, Oxford: Blackwell.

Nussbaum, Martha (1996) 'Patriotism and Cosmopolitanism', in Joshua Cohen, ed., *For Love of Country: Debating the Limits of Patriotism*, Boston: Beacon.

Nussbaum, Martha (2006) *Frontiers of Justice: Disability, Nationality, Species Membership*, Cambridge MA: Harvard University Press.

Nussbaum, Martha (2013) *Political Emotions: Why Love Matters for Justice*, Cambridge MA: Harvard University Press.

Oldenquist, Andrew (1982) 'Loyalties', *Journal of Philosophy* 79 (4), 173–93.

Parkinson, Robert (2016) *The Common Cause: Creating Race and Nation in the American Revolution*, Chapel Hill NC: University of North Carolina Press.

Patten, Alan (1996) 'The Republican Critique of Liberalism', *British Journal of Political Science* 26 (1), 25–44.

Pauer-Studer, Herlinde and J. David Velleman (2015) *Konrad Morgen: The Conscience of a Nazi Judge*, New York: Palgrave Macmillan.

Pettit, Philip (1997) *Republicanism: A Theory of Freedom and Government*, Oxford: Oxford University Press.

Pettit, Philip (2016) 'The Globalized Republican Ideal', *Global Justice: Theory Practice Rhetoric* 9 (1), 47–68.

Plato (1961) *Collected Dialogues*, ed. Edith Hamilton and Huntington Cairns, Princeton: Princeton University Press.

Price, Richard (1789) *A Discourse on the Love of Our Country*, second edition, London, printed for T. Cadell.

Rawls, John (1971) *A Theory of Justice*, Oxford: Oxford University Press.

Renan, Ernest (1939) 'What is a Nation?', in A. Zimmern, ed., *Modern Political Doctrines*, London: Oxford University Press. (Lecture originally delivered in 1882.)

Rorty, Richard (1998) *Achieving Our Country: Leftist Thought in 20th-Century America*, Cambridge MA: Harvard University Press.

Rousseau, Jean-Jacques (1761) *A Project for Perpetual Peace*, London, printed for M. Cooper.

Rousseau, Jean-Jacques (1911) *Emile*, London: Dent.

Rousseau, Jean-Jacques (1987) *Basic Political Writings*, Indianapolis: Hackett.

Rummel, R. J. (1994) *Death by Government*, New Brunswick NJ: Transaction Publishers.

Sample, Ruth J. (2003) *Exploitation*, Lanham MD: Rowman and Littlefield.

Sandel, Michael (1982) *Liberalism and the Limits of Justice*, Cambridge: Cambridge University Press.

Scheffler, Samuel (2001) *Boundaries and Allegiances: Problems of Justice and Responsibility in Liberal Thought*, Oxford: Oxford University Press.

Scheffler, Samuel (2010) *Equality and Tradition: Questions of Value in Moral and Political Theory*, New York: Oxford University Press.

Seck, Sara (2013) 'Transnational Judicial and Non-Judicial Remedies for Corporate Human Rights Harms', *Windsor Yearbook of Access to Justice* 31 (1), 177–95.

Sen, Amartya (2006) *Identity and Violence: The Illusion of Destiny*, New York: Norton.

Shue, Henry (1993) 'Subsistence Emissions and Luxury Emissions', *Law and Policy* 15 (1), 39–59.

Singer, Peter (2002) *One World*, New Haven: Yale University Press.

Skinner, Quentin (1998) *Liberty Before Liberalism*, Cambridge: Cambridge University Press.

Stilz, Anna (2009) *Liberal Loyalty: Freedom, Obligation, and the State*, Princeton: Princeton University Press.

Tamir, Yael (1993) *Liberal Nationalism*, Princeton: Princeton University Press.

Taylor, Charles (1989) 'Cross-Purposes: The Liberal-Communitarian Debate', in Nancy L. Rosenblum, ed., *Liberalism and the Moral Life*, Cambridge MA: Harvard University Press.

Taylor, Charles (1991) 'What's Wrong with Negative Liberty?', in David Miller, ed., *Liberty*, Oxford: Oxford University Press.

Tolstoy, Leo (1894) 'On Patriotism', available at www.nonresistance.org.

Tolstoy, Leo (1900) 'Patriotism and Government', available at www.nonresistance.org.

Valentini, Laura (2011) 'Coercion and Global Justice', *American Political Science Review* 105 (1), 205–20.

Varouxakis, Georgios (2006) ' "Patriotism", "Cosmopolitanism", and "Humanity" in Victorian Political Thought', *European Journal of Political Theory* 5, 100–18.

Vernon, Richard (2010), *Cosmopolitan Regard: Political Membership and Global Justice*, Cambridge: Cambridge University Press.

Viroli, Maurizio (1995) *For Love of Country: An Essay on Patriotism and Nationalism*, Oxford: Clarendon Press.

Waldron, Jeremy (1993) *Liberal Rights*, Cambridge: Cambridge University Press.

Walzer, Michael (1987) *Interpretation and Social Criticism*, Cambridge MA: Harvard University Press.

Walzer, Michael (1988) *The Company of Critics*, New York: Basic Books.

Weber, Eugen (1976) *Peasants into Frenchmen: The Modernization of Rural France, 1870–1914*, Stanford: Stanford University Press.

Weber, Max (1946) 'Politics as a Vocation', in H. H. Gerth and C. Wright Mills, eds, *From Max Weber*, New York: Oxford University Press (first published 1919).

White, Stuart (2003) 'Republicanism, Patriotism, and Global Justice', in Daniel A. Bell and Avner de-Shalit, eds, *Forms of Justice: Critical Perspectives on David Miller's Political Philosophy*, Lanham MD: Rowman and Littlefield.

Williams, Bernard (1981) *Moral Luck*, Cambridge: Cambridge University Press.

Williams, Bernard (2005) *In the Beginning was the Deed: Moralism and Realism in Political Argument*, Princeton: Princeton University Press.

Winch, Peter (1958) *The Idea of a Social Science*, London: Routledge.

Wolf, Susan (2015) *The Variety of Values: Essays on Morality, Meaning, and Love*, Oxford: Oxford University Press.

Young, Iris Marion (1990) *Justice and the Politics of Difference*, Princeton: Princeton University Press.

Index